Working with Traits

Working with Traits

Psychotherapy of
Personality Disorders

Joel Paris, M.D.

JASON ARONSON INC.
Northvale, New Jersey
London

This book was set in 11 pt. New Century Schoolbook by Alabama Book Composition of Deatsville, Alabama, and printed and bound by Book-mart Press, Inc. of North Bergen, New Jersey.

Library of Congress Cataloging-in-Publication Data

Paris, Joel, 1940–
    Working with traits : psychotherapy of personality disorders /
Joel Paris.
        p. cm.
    Includes bibliographical references and index.
    ISBN 0–7657–0096–4 (alk. paper)
    1. Personality disorders—Treatment. I. Title.
    [DNLM: 1. Personality Disorders—therapy. 2. Personality.
3. Psychotherapy—methods. WM 190 P232w 1997]
RC554.P373 1997
616.85'8—dc21
DNLM/DLC
for Library of Congress   97-18482

Printed in the United States of America on acid-free paper. Jason Aronson Inc. offers books and cassettes. For information and catalog write to Jason Aronson Inc., 230 Livingston Street, Northvale, New Jersey 07647-1731. Or visit our website: http://www.aronson.com

To my wife, Rosalind Paris

Contents

Acknowledgments

No book can be written without a great deal of help. I benefited from the input of two readers who accepted the labor of reviewing the entire manuscript, both in its early stages and in later versions. My wife, Rosalind Paris, helped me present my ideas coherently and write this book in a user-friendly style. My longtime research colleague, Hallie Zweig-Frank, challenged many of my conclusions and helped to make sure that my ideas follow logically from each other.

Three colleagues provided additional assistance. Carl Auerbach read early versions of Chapters 4, 5, and 6. Danny Frank read a draft of Chapter 3. Joe Meagher provided documentation of borderline pathology in Lady Caroline Lamb, as quoted in Chapter 5.

I would also like to acknowledge those who specifically supported me in the project of writing this book. The time required to write the text was provided by the Department of Psychiatry of the Sir Mortimer B. Davis–Jewish General Hospital and its Psychiatrist-in-Chief, Dr. Phillip Beck, as well as by the Department of Psychiatry of McGill University and its former Chairman, Dr. Gilbert Pinard. The librarians at the Institute of Community and Family Psychiatry, Ruth Stillman and Judy Grossman, provided indispensable help in obtaining references.

Finally, I would like to offer special thanks to the dedicatee of this book—my wife, who encouraged me to enter psychiatry and who, over the years, has provided consistent and much needed support for my career.

Introduction

THE PURPOSE OF THIS BOOK

The treatment of patients with personality disorders is arduous. It is also far from consistently successful. It is therefore not very surprising that clinicians working with this population often seek advice from experts. However, expert consultants tend to do better at explaining the factors behind personality pathology than at instructing therapists to change problematic behavior.

This book will therefore aim to be a practical guide to the clinician working with personality-disordered patients. It will differ from previous books on the subject in two important ways. First, its method will be based on a broad and comprehensive etiological theory. Second, its approach to treatment will be consistent with the research literature.

In order to develop systematic ways of treating personality disorders, we need to understand their origins. This book will underscore how much we still need to learn about the complex pathways to developing personality pathology. Traditionally, clinicians have espoused the theory that problems in adult behavior depend largely on the quality of childhood experiences. The key to psychotherapy then becomes the uncovering and working through of the past. These assumptions are ubiquitous, and many of our patients share them. Yet the reader of this book will be surprised by how little evidence there is for these ideas.

At best, they are half-truths. At worst, they are seriously misleading.

Life histories do affect personality but to a lesser extent than we think. The present is only partially determined by the past. The primacy of early childhood experience has become a dogma that fails to address other important influences on personality structure: constitution, adult life experiences, and the social environment. These additional factors help to explain why knowledge of the past is insufficient, by itself, to produce change in the present.

Working with troubled people can be a moving experience. As therapists, we are privileged to be trusted with the opportunity to address the human condition. Psychotherapy is also an art form. The language of therapy is rich in metaphor, and good therapists are more like poets than scientists.

Nonetheless, this book will attempt to take a hardheaded, empirical view of its subject. Too many books about psychotherapy have relied exclusively on clinical wisdom, presenting little in the way of data. This fault might be explained by a lack of knowledge. We cannot offer more than a broad outline of the causes of personality pathology. Nor do we have more than a handful of clinical trials showing that psychotherapy helps personality-disordered patients. Still, therapists must be committed in principle to the idea that most clinical questions can eventually be answered through research. In another decade or two, we should know a great deal more about the etiology of personality disorders and their treatment.

The effectiveness of any therapeutic method can only be demonstrated by empirical data. This involves "manualizing" techniques and then subjecting them to systematic clinical trials. Unfortunately, most psychotherapy research concerns short-term interventions; very few studies have been conducted on long-term psychotherapy. This lacuna reflects the inevitable methodological and logistic problems in studying lengthy and complex treatments.

Therapists can hardly afford to wait fifty years until sufficient data are collected to draw conclusions. We are faced every day with patients who have a legitimate need for our help. We cannot tell them to wait until we obtain a better understanding of personality disorders or of the mechanisms of psychotherapy. Rather, we must continue doing our best while we wait for better methods of treatment to be developed.

What this book offers is an approach that is, at the very least, consistent with the research literature. Ultimately, the practice of psychotherapy should be firmly based on empirical findings. In the future, instead of having "schools" of therapy, we will develop a generally agreed-upon and highly eclectic method of practice that will be reasonably standard for all practitioners. At present, since so many of the most important questions about the conduct of therapy have not yet been subjected to empirical study, psychotherapists must continue to rely on intuition and clinical skills.

In spite of all these limitations, psychotherapy research has many useful things to tell us about the overall efficacy of psychological treatments. Ideally, clinicians should be as conversant with research on their methods as physicians are with studies of drugs. Moreover, some of the implications of empirical research are rather encouraging for therapists. We will discuss this subject in detail later in the book, but a few findings are worth mentioning here:

1. *Finding*: Most methods of psychotherapy yield similar results.
   Implication: There is no one right way to conduct treatment.

2. *Finding*: Experience has a weak relationship to outcome.
   Implication: Even if you are just starting out as a therapist, you are probably better than you think you are.

3. *Finding*: Psychotherapy is more effective in treating symptoms than in modifying personality traits.

Implication: The goals for treating personality-disordered patients should be modest and attainable.

HOW I CAME TO THE CONCLUSIONS IN THIS BOOK

I have described a troubling gap between research and practice in psychotherapy. In many ways, this problem parallels the trajectory of my own career. I would therefore like to share with the reader some of my experiences.

Thirty years ago, I trained as a clinical psychiatrist, developing a strong interest in psychotherapy. In the first ten years after my residency, I spent many hours treating personality-disordered patients in long-term therapy. My results, like those of most clinicians, were variable. The outcomes ranged from gratifying successes to complete failures, with most cases falling somewhere in the middle. Like many young therapists, I assumed that the results were limited by my lack of experience and that with time I would be able to accomplish much more. In fact, my outcomes eventually *did* improve. However, this was largely because I became more streetwise, learning to choose the patients most likely to get better!

Over time, I began to wonder whether I was working with an adequate theoretical model. Like many other therapists, I read books, went to conferences, talked to my colleagues, and tried to become conversant with all current theoretical models. Each time I was exposed to a new idea, I would try to apply it to my clinical work. In spite of my many initial bursts of enthusiasm, no theory adequately accounted for what I was seeing in my practice.

Eventually, I concluded that speculations drawn from case material are not the ideal way to advance knowledge. As a result, I developed a second career as a researcher. I was fortunate enough to find colleagues who were interested in the same questions that had troubled me. Over the following decade, I became involved with a research group studying the etiology and outcome of personality disorders.

Research also changed many of my clinical beliefs. I no longer saw the narratives emerging from therapy as accurate accounts of the past. Moreover, I came to the conclusion that childhood experiences cannot, by themselves, account for the development of personality disorders, which derive from interactions among biological, psychological, and social factors. Although everyone pays lip service to the biopsychosocial model, it should be acknowledged as the only approach that adequately addresses the complexity of psychopathology.

Finally, research changed my approach to evaluating treatment. I became converted to the principles of evidence-based medicine, and could no longer accept the statements of authorities at face value.

PREVIOUS BOOKS ON THE PSYCHOTHERAPY OF PERSONALITY DISORDERS

The methods of therapy to be described in this book may seem different from the recommendations of other writers. Yet I hope that many readers may agree with my own belief that I have described with fair accuracy how the best practitioners *really* conduct psychotherapy. We can account for this paradox by assuming that the ideas in this book represent what many experienced therapists actually *do* with their patients, as opposed to what they *say* they do.

Most psychotherapists begin by applying the specific techniques in which they have been trained. Over time, they discover their limitations and then evolve, by trial and error, modifications that work better. As a result, they become more eclectic, so their methods increasingly cut across the schools of therapy. Thus, experienced psychodynamic therapists will focus less exclusively on interpretations and will provide more confrontation and advice. Behavior therapists will focus less on symptoms and will become expert at treating the whole person. In other words, all good therapists, no matter where they start from, end up doing what works.

In this respect, it is not surprising that the ideas presented here will not be completely original. Rather, this book aims to integrate my conclusions about the etiology and treatment of the personality disorders with those of many other writers. I am therefore strongly indebted to a number of predecessors.

Benjamin (1993) used an interpersonal theory of personality as the basis for a therapy designed for personality-disordered patients. Millon and Davis (1996) applied a biosocial model of the personality disorders to their treatment. Stone (1993) knitted together many theoretical traditions into a uniquely eclectic approach to management. Burks and Rubenstein (1979) described the importance of temperamental differences between patients in psychotherapy. Beck and Freeman (1990) developed a cognitive-behavioral theory of personality disorders based on temperamental theory which is very similar to my own. Ryle's (1997) model of borderline pathology also resembles the one to be presented here. Finally, Linehan's (1993) cognitive-behavioral model for patients with borderline personality disorder has had a particularly strong influence on my ideas.

My theoretical model of the etiology of personality disorders has been developed in detail in a previous book (Paris 1996). Here, I briefly review that theory but focus on the application of the model to clinical practice.

THE CHALLENGE OF TREATING PERSONALITY-DISORDERED PATIENTS

The *Diagnostic and Statistical Manual of Mental Disorders, 4th Edition DSM-IV* (American Psychiatric Association 1994) defines a personality disorder as an enduring pattern of inner experience or behavior that deviates markedly from the expectations of the individual's culture. This pattern must be manifest in at least two of the following sectors: cognition, affect, interpersonal functioning, or impulse control. In addition, the pattern must be inflexible or pervasive across a broad range of personal or social situations. It must lead to clinically significant distress or impairment in social, occupational, or other forms of functioning. Finally, the pattern must be stable and of long duration, with an onset that can be traced back at least to adolescence or early adulthood. These characteristics all describe *chronicity*. It is therefore not surprising that personality-disordered patients resist change.

Several trends have worked against the development of therapy for patients with personality disorders. Some clinicians are dismissive of the clinical significance of personality pathology, sometimes using the pejorative term *worried well* to describe these patients. Other clinicians avoid diagnosing personality disorders entirely, and describe patients' pathology strictly on the basis of symptoms that could respond to medication. Moreover, as psychotherapies are becoming shorter and more symptom-oriented, any disorders that require longer therapy receive a lower priority. Many clinicians are reluctant to invest scarce and increasingly expensive human resources on a patient group that frequently fails to respond to their efforts.

The danger is that all these developments will lead to the abandonment of patients with personality disorders. Yet, patients with Axis II diagnoses (personality disorders) suffer no less than do those with Axis I diagnoses (symptomatic disorders). What arguments can we use to justify investing our therapeutic resources? Although the successful treatment of maladaptive personality traits usually requires a longer course of psychotherapy than Axis I symptoms, taking the time to treat these patients is ultimately justified by their suffering.

In recent years, many therapists have been attracted to pharmacological treatments that are perceived as cost-effective alternatives to talking therapies. Most clinicians, even if they are not themselves physicians, have ready access to medical consultation. However, once the consultative process is launched, it is almost inevitable that the patient ends up receiving some form of medication. This trend has had both positive and negative effects. Some patients with personality disorders do benefit from pharmacological treatment for major depression or dysthymia. On the other hand, as compared to cases of "pure" depression, patients with Axis II diagnoses have a relatively poor response to antidepressant medications (Shea et al. 1992).

By and large, all drugs presently available for patients with personality disorders have only marginal effects (Paris 1996). Rather, like aspirin for pain, medications take the edge off psychic distress but do not address underlying pathology. The idea that the newer types of antidepressants might change personality traits (Kramer 1993) remains an interesting but unproven hypothesis.

Some clinicians may even be losing sight of the value of psychotherapy. This is particularly true in depression, for which pharmacological treatment has become predominant. Certainly many patients with personality disorders come for treatment because they feel depressed. This is not surprising, given the roots of many depressions in personality structure. It should therefore not be surprising that addressing interpersonal problems, in addition to symptoms, usually leads to better treatment (Klerman and Weissman 1993). It is also possible that treating comorbid Axis II disorders may offer a better chance of reducing the high relapse rate of depressive illness. The treatment of personality disorders must continue to lie at the core of the psychotherapeutic enterprise.

WORKING WITH TRAITS

The method of therapy in this book is based on the following principles:

1. All individuals have a characteristic personality trait profile.
2. Traits are shaped by both genetic factors and experience.
3. Personality disorders are maladaptive exaggerations of these traits.
4. Psychosocial factors determine whether traits develop into disorders.

Consistent with these principles, the goals for psychotherapy
are:

1. To reverse the process by which traits develop into disorders.
2. To demonstrate to patients how they use traits maladaptively.
3. To develop ways to use existing traits more adaptively.
4. To use traits more flexibly and to widen behavioral repertoires.

This method differs from most previous approaches in three
ways. It does not assume that all patients with personality
disorders are suitable for psychotherapy; rather, it identifies a
treatable minority who can make the best use of psychological
interventions. It does not assume that psychological insight is
the primary focus of treatment; rather, it recognizes that understanding is only one step toward change. It does not pretend to
be neutral about maladaptive behavior; rather, it acknowledges
that psychotherapy has an overt agenda for increasing social
adaptation and prescribing specific changes.

In this book, we will present a two-pronged approach to psychotherapy. The most effective methods of treatment are eclectic
and involve an integration of psychodynamic and cognitive-
behavioral principles. We can help patients understand their
personal histories but must still offer them a technology for
change.

THE ARGUMENT OF THE CHAPTERS

Chapter 1 begins by reviewing the nature of normal personality.
We all have specific personality traits, that is, consistent patterns of behavior, emotion, and cognition. These individual
differences in personality are determined by biology, life experiences, and social influences.

Chapter 2 addresses the question of how traits develop into

disorders. Personality disorders are maladaptive and amplified forms of normal traits. We will critique the primacy of childhood experience and develop an alternative theory in which biological, psychological, and social factors influence trait amplification.

Chapter 3 examines what research tells us about psychotherapy in general and about the therapy of personality disorders in particular. Success usually depends more on the nature of patients than on the qualities of therapists. Moreover, outcome tends not to depend on specific techniques. Finally, personality pathology requires longer periods of treatment than do other symptoms. These findings are both good news and bad news. On the one hand, clinicians need not blame themselves for insoluble problems. On the other hand, they may have to be satisfied with limited results.

Chapter 4 applies the etiological model of the personality disorders developed in the first two chapters to their treatment. This approach can most succinctly be described as working *with* traits rather than against them. Thus, the goal of therapy with personality-disordered patients is to make personality more adaptive by moderating traits and learning to use them in new ways. The technique of therapy with personality-disordered patients has both psychodynamic and cognitive-behavioral components. Psychodynamic interpretations provide validation for the patient's life experience and help place the patient's problems in historical context. To produce behavioral change, however, the most important therapeutic interventions are confrontations, analysis of maladaptive behaviors, and the development of adaptive alternatives.

In the second part of the book, these principles will be applied to the therapy of five specific categories of personality disorder, using the *DSM-IV* classification. Although this system has many limitations, it remains a convenient way of describing clinical prototypes. However, although Axis II divides personality disorders into three clusters, there will be no separate chapter on the disorders in Cluster A of Axis II, since so few of these patients are suitable for psychotherapy. Similarly, there will be no chapter on antisocial personality disorder, a Cluster B category that is famously resistant to treatment.

In each of the chapters on specific disorders, I will relate the disorder to its underlying traits and then suggest how to modify those traits. I will also illustrate these principles with case vignettes. Each vignette will be organized as follows: history, suitability for therapy, alliance and structure, interventions (confrontations of maladaptive behaviors, the psychodynamic prong, the cognitive-behavioral prong, making better use of existing traits), and outcome.

The vignettes will, of course, disguise any identifying data about patients. However, in contrast to certain other books about psychotherapy, I will not attempt to disguise the *outcome* of treatment. The treatment of patients with personality disorders does not always yield dramatic results, and clinicians must often be satisfied with partial recoveries. The cases will therefore be chosen not to impress the reader with inspiring narratives describing "cures," but to reflect with some accuracy the realities of clinical practice.

Chapter 5 applies the model to borderline personality disorder. Reflecting the great interest of clinicians and researchers in this condition and the size of the literature on borderline pathology, this will be the longest chapter in the book. The treatment of borderline patients will be shown to depend on modifying underlying traits of impulsivity and emotional instability.

Chapter 6 applies the model to narcissistic personality disorder. It will discuss the relationship of narcissistic traits to the social environment. The method of treatment focuses on ways to modify grandiosity and entitlement in the patient's current relationships.

Chapter 7 applies the model to histrionic personality disorder. The method focuses on the modification of excessive extraversion.

Chapter 8 applies the model to avoidant and dependent

personality disorders. The method focuses on modifying anxious temperament.

Chapter 9 applies the model to compulsive personality disorder. The method focuses on making compulsive traits work for patients.

Chapter 10 summarizes the conclusions of the book. Personality traits are a limiting factor for all forms of therapy. There are several ways by which the model proposed in this book might be tested. Finally, I will offer a vision of the future of psychotherapy.

1

The Nature
of Personality

WHAT IS PERSONALITY?

People react to life's challenges in different ways. All of us have unique behavioral patterns that are fairly consistent from one situation to another. These individual characteristics define what is popularly called *personality*.

Individual differences in personality lead to different life choices. Thus, some people will only be happy if they marry and have children, while others are content living alone. Some people need to find work with a high level of personal interaction, while others are most productive in an atmosphere of solitude and serenity.

There is room for all kinds of people in the world. The crucial point is that individuals with every type of personality must find their own niches. Since variations in personality structures lead to variable ways of managing life, the goals of therapy must be different for different people.

Psychologists make use of a more precise terminology to describe these individual differences. Personality *traits* are consistent patterns of behavior, emotion, and cognition. When traits are independent of each other, they are referred to as *dimensions* of personality.

Personality dimensions can be broad, describing the most

universal and normal characteristics of personality. They can also be narrow, describing more specific aspects of personality, particularly those that are likely to be pathological.

One of the broadest and most basic personality dimensions is *extraversion* vs. *introversion* (Eysenck 1991, McCrae and Costa 1990). This construct was first used about seventy-five years ago (Jung 1920). It describes differences between those who are generally outgoing and those who are more likely to prefer their own company. Extraverts require a high level of interpersonal stimulation and therefore need to be around people. Introverts function better at lower levels of stimulation and therefore need more time alone. Each end of this continuum has its advantages and disadvantages; most people fall somewhere in the middle of the distribution.

A second broad dimension of personality is *neuroticism*. This trait describes differences between people who worry a good deal and those who hardly worry at all. High levels of neuroticism are associated with a number of mental disorders, particularly depression and somatization (Kirmayer et al. 1994). Although worrying too much can increase the risk for psychopathology, those who are low on neuroticism may be unrealistically optimistic, even in the face of serious difficulties. There are times in life when vigilance is called for, and some degree of neuroticism is therefore necessary and healthy.

Extraversion and neuroticism are basic to most classifications of personality. Other models use more dimensions. Eysenck (1991) added a third, which he called *psychoticism*, a trait that really reflects impulsivity, not psychosis. The most influential schema in contemporary American psychology is the Five Factor Model (McCrae and Costa 1990). In addition to extraversion and neuroticism, this system describes three other personality dimensions: conscientiousness, openness to experience, and agreeableness. This scheme has been shown to provide a broad profile of normal personality as well as of personality disorders (Costa and Widiger 1993).

Cloninger (1987) has proposed a somewhat different classification using three dimensions: *harm avoidance* (the extent to which we avoid the negative consequences of behavior), *reward dependence* (how much we care what other people think), and *novelty seeking* (how much we need to find new sources of stimulation). Recently, Cloninger and colleagues (1993) have added a fourth dimension of *persistence* to the model.

All these systems use a few broad dimensions to describe normal personality. It is not clear, however, whether these dimensions are the best way to describe pathology. Livesley and colleagues (1994) have applied a scheme using eighteen dimensions to describe the symptoms of personality disorders. Although complex, this kind of profile could be useful for clinicians in describing patients.

As described in *DSM-IV*, it is only when behaviors are used rigidly and maladaptively and when they significantly interfere with functioning that we can diagnose a personality disorder. By themselves, personality traits are not pathological but are often adaptive. As suggested by Millon and Davis (1996), traits function rather like an immune system. The challenges presented to us by the environment must be dealt with, and our traits function to process the impact of life events. However, like the immune system, personality structures can be overwhelmed by environmental challenges, particularly when insults are severe and continuous.

A crucial aspect of trait theory concerns the significance of individual differences in personality. Traits are essentially built-in adaptations, designed to cope with the most frequently expected environmental challenges. However, every organism has to cope with an environment that is highly variable. Differences in personality are therefore alternate strategies, which can be more adaptive under one set of circumstances and less adaptive under another set of circumstances.

Let us consider two examples of this principle. Shyness is defined by the strength of a child's anxiety when exposed to strangers. This trait, also called *behavioral inhibition*, is known to have a strong genetic component (Kagan 1994). As everyone who has this characteristic knows, shyness can be painful. Why, then, does the trait remain in the gene pool? The most likely explanation is that social avoidance is adaptive under certain conditions, that is, when strangers present a real threat. In fact, through most of history, strangers *have* been dangerous, and some of them continue to be so. The trait becomes maladaptive in those modern settings where threats from outsiders are rare and shyness interferes with peer relationships, leading to a dysfunctional degree of social isolation.

A second example concerns impulsivity. Under conditions of immediate external danger, rapid responses are more adaptive than slow ones. Throughout most of human history, dangerous situations have been the rule, not the exception. In modern society, impulsive traits become maladaptive when rapid responses are mobilized in the absence of any realistic danger and impulsivity interferes with rational judgment.

THE STABILITY OF PERSONALITY

Personality traits appear early in life and remain stable over time. For the most part, personality changes surprisingly little between the ages of 18 and 60 (McCrae and Costa 1990). Thus, those who are extraverted or introverted as adolescents will remain so in their old age. The same applies to those who are highly neurotic, conscientious, agreeable, or open to experience.

The main exception to this rule is impulsivity. We all become less impulsive as we grow older. In a prospective study of normal men who had attended Harvard University fifty years ago, Vaillant (1977) found that most impulsive behaviors fell off with time, whereas other (nonimpulsive) behavioral patterns tended to continue.

These findings in normal samples are paralleled by follow-up studies of patients with impulsive personality diagnoses. Thus, disorders in the "dramatic" cluster on Axis II, particularly antisocial personality (Black et al. 1995) and borderline personality (Paris 1993a), show a marked decline in prevalence after middle age. These reductions in impulsivity might be explained by structural or neurochemical changes in the brain over time that reduce impulsive behaviors in middle age.

The overall stability of personality is not just a matter of biology. It also reflects feedback loops between genes and environment. Personality traits tend to elicit environmental responses that reinforce them. This is particularly true during childhood. Research shows that impulsive children are more likely to be beaten, which, in turn, can make them even more impulsive (Rutter and Quinton 1984). Anxious children are more likely to be overprotected, which, in turn, can make them even more anxious (Kagan 1994). Similar feedback mechanisms probably contribute to the stability of personality in adults (Wachtel 1993).

There is, however, a limit to the shaping of traits by experience. Because personality is strongly influenced by genes, an introvert can never become an extravert, nor can an extravert become an introvert. It is the *degree* of introversion or extraversion in any individual that is open to environmental influence.

THE ORIGINS OF PERSONALITY

Temperament

As anyone who has worked in a newborn nursery knows, infants differ from each other in how active they are, how sociable they are, how easily they get upset, and how readily they can be calmed down. These differences constitute what we call *temperament*— behavioral dispositions already present at birth.

Within a normal range, infantile temperament predicts little about adult personality. Few consistent findings emerge from long-term follow-up studies of children with different temperamental dispositions. The most consistent predictor is a "difficult" temperament. This describes infants who become easily upset and who are hard to calm down. Difficult infants are statistically more likely to develop psychopathology later in life (Chess and Thomas 1990), but the majority never develop any mental disorder.

The explanation of these findings is that there is not enough variation in temperament among normal children to account for the vulnerability to mental disorders. *Extreme* temperaments are much better predictors of psychopathology. Two longitudinal studies have been following such children. Maziade and colleagues (1990) have been studying a cohort of children who were unusually difficult as infants. Kagan (1994) has been following a group of children with extreme levels of shyness. Although we do not yet have information on these cohorts as adults, both show an increased risk of developing psychological symptoms later in childhood and in adolescence.

Other research evidence also shows that children with unusually problematical temperamental characteristics are more likely to have trouble later in life. Longitudinal studies suggest that children with increased fearfulness and irritability are more likely to become neurotic, children with increased activity level and positive affect become more extraverted, and children with attentional persistence become more conscientious, while children who are easily prone to distress have more difficulties with attachment (Rothbart and Ahadi 1994).

Temperament "bends the twig," but it does not determine the shape of the tree. Thus genetics sets a limit on individual variability while the environment determines the final form of personality. In general, stable personality traits only emerge from complex interactions between temperament and social learning (Rutter 1987).

Children with different temperamental dispositions respond to the same parental behaviors in different ways. Siblings raised in the same family develop different personalities and can be almost as different in their personality traits as perfect strangers (Dunn and Plomin 1990). One explanation for this observation involves genetic differences. In addition, personality is strongly influenced by the social context outside the family (Millon 1993).

Because the environment of each child is unique, personality is not solely determined by parental input.

These findings should not surprise most parents. Even mental health professionals have had the experience that, in spite of their best intentions, their children are not very malleable! The role of temperament has been embodied in a witticism: "the mother of one child believes in the environment; the mother of two children believes in the genes."

The Genetics of Personality

The broadest personality dimensions have been examined in large-scale studies conducted in cultures all over the world (Eysenck 1991). By and large, the results show that the same traits are found in people everywhere. These findings clearly support the biological grounding of personality. This conclusion is also supported by associations between traits and biological markers, including blood groupings (Eysenck 1991), as well as neurochemical activity (Cloninger 1987, Coccaro et al. 1989, Siever and Davis 1991).

However, the strongest evidence for a genetic component in personality comes from twin studies. This method provides the bedrock data on which the discipline of behavioral genetics (Plomin et al. 1990) has been built. Measuring the heritability of traits in twins allows us to make a quantitative estimate of the contribution of genes to personality.

Genetic factors are estimated by comparing identical or monozygotic (MZ) twins and fraternal or dizygotic (DZ) twins. A large number of studies show that MZ twins have much higher concordances for most personality traits than do DZ twins. A statistical measure called *heritability* is derived from this data, and can be used to estimate the percentage of variation accounted for by genetic factors (Carey and DiLalla 1994). Most personality traits have moderate heritabilities, usually between 40 and 50 percent (Livesley et al. 1993, Plomin et al. 1990). In other words: nearly half the variance in most dimensions of personality can be attributed to the genes.

Twins separated at birth provide an even more striking demonstration of the heritability of personality. The Minnesota Twin Study examined personality traits in MZ and DZ twins raised together and apart (Bergeman et al. 1993, Tellegen et al. 1988). Correlations between scores on a personality measure (the eleven dimensions of the Multidimensional Personality Questionnaire) for MZ twins were just as high whether the twins were raised in the same family or separated at birth. Dizygotic twins showed surprisingly little similarity in personality.

Although most personality traits are heritable, some are more heritable than others. One of the most consistent findings is that extraversion and neuroticism are strongly inherited. However, in the Five Factor Model, agreeableness is less under genetic influence than the other four dimensions (Bergeman et al. 1993). The Minnesota Twin Study, as well as another large community study (Livesley et al. 1993), found only a moderate (about 30 percent) heritability for dimensions of social closeness and intimacy. Livesley and colleagues also found differential inheritance for other traits: high heritabilities (above 50 percent) for callousness, identity problems, narcissism, oppositionality, and social avoidance, but lower heritabilities (less than 30 percent) for conduct problems, self-harm, and submissiveness.

The mechanisms by which genetic factors influence personality are complex. Personality traits are usually influenced not by single genes, but by interactions among many genes. As scientists map the human genome, we are beginning to read reports in the media about specific genes for specific traits. For example, one recent report (Benjamin et al. 1996) suggested that Cloninger's dimension of novelty seeking can be located at a specific site on a specific chromosome. However, it is hard to imagine that a single gene could control anything as complex as a personality trait. More likely, these mappings describe one gene among many that influence, directly or indirectly, the development of personality.

The Role of Experience

How does the environment shape personality? According to the model of "social learning" (Bandura 1977), this process involves two mechanisms. First, children are positively reinforced for some kinds of behavior and negatively reinforced for other kinds of behavior. Second, children imitate the behavior of important adults in their lives.

Children develop their personality traits early on and maintain the same characteristics later. This does not prove, however, that early experiences are more important than later ones. Rather, as discussed above, the early onset and stability of personality traits is largely due to genetic factors.

Nevertheless, over 50 percent of the variance in personality traits is not inherited. Thus, behavioral genetic research actually demonstrates the importance of the environment. However, the most surprising finding of twin research concerns the source of these non-genetic influences: the environmental contribution to personality is largely *unshared*, that is, not related to living in the same family.

How can we explain the importance of the unshared environment in personality formation? It may be that children in the same family have different experiences. Thus, siblings might receive differential treatment from their parents, as in the phenomenon of scapegoating. Differences in birth order could lead each sibling to seek a different niche in the family (Sulloway 1996). Probably the most important factor, however, involves traits. Temperamental differences lead each child to perceive the same experiences differently, so that a family can be "good enough" for one child, yet grossly inadequate for another. Thus, whether parents provide a good "fit" for each child is the most important mechanism determining whether parenting is pathogenic (Kendler 1996). Finally, the unshared environment also includes experiences outside the nuclear family that affect personality (Reiss et al. 1992). These influences include attachments to extended family members, socioeconomic circumstances, culture, the availability of social networks, and the cohesiveness of the social community (Paris 1996).

In summary, research contradicts the impression we get from our clinical work that early childhood experience is the primary factor in personality development. Under the influence, no doubt, of our own expectations, as well as of a culture that believes that people are largely products of their upbringing, we are tempted to agree with our patients that an unhappy childhood is the main reason for their problems.

There is no doubt that many patients have had more than their share of misery as children. However, the associations between negative experiences in early childhood and adult psychopathology are misleading if they fail to take into account why different children respond differently to the same circumstances. This phenomenon is called *resilience*.

Children have the capacity to emerge unscathed from the worst parenting experiences (Rutter 1989). For every patient we see with negative experiences, there could be ten non-patients who are functioning reasonably well in spite of an unhappy childhood. We need also not assume that traumatic experiences affect people for their whole lives. Rather, pathological sequelae are most likely to result from the cumulative effects of *many* negative experiences (Rutter and Rutter 1993).

Gene-environment Interactions

Genes and environment produce their effects through a feedback loop that reflects their many points of interaction. For example, children influence the quality of their environment and shape the responses of others to their traits (Scarr and McCartney 1983). Thus, a highly intelligent child will spend much more time in intellectual activities and seek out an enriched environment. In fact, children with any specific interests tend to search, often outside their immediate families, for people and activities, to help them develop their natural abilities.

Another point of interaction between genes and environment concerns the quality of parenting. Successfully raising children requires flexibility toward their needs. We are more likely to be able to bring up our children without difficulty if they have "easy" temperaments. Moreover, all parents find some trait profiles in their children more manageable than others. Problems arise when there is a poor fit between parental expectations and the temperament of the child (Chess and Thomas 1990). Temperamental abnormalities become amplified when they create difficulties for parents and peers. A child with a difficult temperament will also be more susceptible to environmental stressors (Kendler 1995).

DEFENSE MECHANISMS AS TRAITS

The idea that personality structures have a defensive function can be traced back to the ideas of Wilhelm Reich (1933). Reich saw personality characteristics as defenses against inner conflicts, as "character armor" that must first be removed before a therapist can resolve and work through underlying neurotic problems. This view of personality traits has permeated the psychodynamic literature.

Consistent with the literature reviewed in this chapter, we are arguing that personality traits are *not* defenses. The term *defense mechanisms* is a misleading way of describing patterns of behavior. The concept derives from the idea that overt behaviors mask inner conflicts. However, since behavioral patterns are as likely to be adaptive as maladaptive, defenses would be better described as *coping styles*. In classical psychodynamic theory, everyone has more or less the same intrapsychic structures, and traits function as defenses against these universal needs. If, on the other hand, personality differences are biological givens, they do not need to defend against anything at all, but simply reflect the fact that each individual has a different way of coping.

Instead of seeing traits as defenses, it makes much more sense to assume that defenses are traits. When defense styles are studied empirically, they do in fact behave very much like traits. Thus, in behavioral genetic research, defenses show the same degree of heritability as other personality characteristics (Andrews 1991).

Defense styles reflect the quality of adaptation to the environment. Vaillant (1977) and Vaillant and Vaillant (1990) have shown that mature defenses are associated with better psychological functioning as well as with greater longevity. Interestingly, Vaillant found no association between defense maturity and the quality of childhood experiences. This finding makes sense if we assume that defenses are reflections of personality traits that are under genetic influence.

Researchers on defense styles (e.g., Perry and Cooper 1989, Vaillant 1977) have suggested that defenses can be placed on a hierarchy, from the most immature (such as projection and acting out) to the most mature (such as altruism, humor, and suppression). As people become more mature, they move up this hierarchy. However, as with traits, there are limits as to how much defenses can change. Vaillant studied defense styles over a lifetime in two cohorts of men. He found that those who used immature defenses at age 18 matured over time but tended to remain at a lower level on the hierarchy than those who already used more mature defense styles in adolescence. Personality traits are therefore a limiting factor in how mature people can become.

CLINICAL IMPLICATIONS OF TRAIT THEORY

Psychotherapists should be cautious about routinely attributing personality problems to deficiencies in parenting. Personality traits are an amalgam of constitution and experience. When we see troubled patients, it is tempting to attribute their difficulties to negative childhood experiences. These formulations are, at best, half-truths that fail to do justice to the complexity of development.

In the course of this book I will suggest a different way of understanding and dealing with character traits in psychotherapy. Traits define the individual differences between patients that therapists need to take into account. Thus, each personality type can be defined by a characteristic type of sensitivity to the environment. As therapists, we need to work our way around these sensitivities. Understanding personality traits allows us to adapt psychotherapy to the needs of each individual.

2

The Origins of
Personality Disorders

DEFINITION AND CLASSIFICATION

As discussed in the Introduction, a personality disorder is defined by *DSM-IV* as an enduring pattern of inner experience or behavior that deviates markedly from the expectations of the individual's culture.

Yet, studies in community populations (Livesley et al. 1994) show that there is no sharp cut-off point between normal and pathological personality. Therefore, disorders can be understood as amplifications of normal traits. Personality traits used in rigid, maladaptive, and inappropriate ways lead to dysfunction in work, relationships, or both. We can only diagnose a personality disorder when traits reach a level at which they compromise the capacity for work or intimacy.

Personality disorders are further classified by *DSM-IV* into ten categories, which can then be grouped into three clusters. Each of these clusters is based on common traits. The A Cluster describes "odd" individuals, including categories of schizoid, schizotypal, and paranoid personality disorder. The B Cluster describes dramatic or impulsive individuals, including categories of antisocial, borderline, narcissistic, and histrionic personality disorder. The C Cluster describes pathologically anxious individuals, including categories of avoidant, dependent, and compulsive personality disorder. Many patients, probably about a third of the total (Loranger 1991, Mulder 1991), fit none of these categories but still meet the overall criteria for a personality disorder, and are therefore classified as "Personality disorder, not otherwise specified."

What determines which type of personality disorder a patient develops? Traditionally, clinicians have assumed that specific psychodynamic and experiential constellations are associated with specific forms of psychopathology. There is little evidence for this view. Trait profiles constitute the vulnerability factors for personality disorders and determine which types of disorder can develop in any individual.

HOW PERSONALITY TRAITS BECOME MALADAPTIVE

When traits become too intense, we can describe them as *amplified*. Traits are most likely to become maladaptive when the same behaviors are applied to every situation. Thus, behaviors that might be adaptive in one context will be used in a global and rigid fashion and applied in inappropriate ways. This results in conflict with other people, which then causes even more trait amplification, creating a positive feedback loop.

To demonstrate how these mechanisms work, let us return to the basic personality dimension of extraversion–introversion. Extraverted children tend to be lively, social, and easily lovable. For most extraverts, these traits work well. However, in the presence of a stressful environment, an extraverted person tends to react by reaching out to others for increased social contact and support. This is still an adaptive response. Yet, when overly amplified, extraversion can become dysfunctional. For example, a child might insist on being the constant center of attention and show protest behaviors when attention is withdrawn. These demanding behaviors eventually produce negative responses. When excessive extraversion causes trouble in many contexts, we see a pattern that begins to correspond to the criteria for impulsive cluster disorders (especially the histrionic and narcissistic categories).

Introverted children can be well focused and relatively autonomous. However, in the presence of a stressful environment, an introverted child will tend to withdraw and seek greater protection from caretakers. If the environment is consistently negative, introversion can become pathologically exaggerated. At this point, social contacts may begin to correspond to a picture of "anxious attachment" (Bowlby 1973). At a further level of amplification, they begin to approximate the criteria for personality disorders in the anxious cluster (especially the dependent and avoidant categories).

GENETIC FACTORS IN THE PERSONALITY DISORDERS

In the previous chapter, we reviewed evidence for genetic factors in normal personality traits. However, by themselves, genes do not cause personality disorders. Rather, biology shapes trait profiles which can develop either in adaptive or maladaptive ways, depending on environmental factors.

Research studies consistently show that personality traits are much more strongly inherited than are personality disorders (McGuffin and Thapar 1992, Nigg and Goldsmith 1994, Paris 1996, Torgersen 1980, 1983, 1984). However, if disorders are amplifications of traits, they should show *some* degree of heritability. Recently, Torgersen (1996) has shown that this is the case. In a large scale study of Norwegian twins, he found that the two most common disorders seen in clinical practice, borderline personality and avoidant personality, each have about a 50 percent level of heritability.

Our present knowledge about the nature of the genetic factors that influence the development of personality disorders is limited. To some extent, this reflects defects in our classification of personality pathology. The categories listed in *DSM-IV* are not based on an etiological theory. At best, the ten diagnoses listed on Axis II are clinically useful labels, which provide a convenient summary of many complex observations. (It can be, for example, a meaningful statement to say, "this patient is a typical border-line.")

Ultimately, however, we need to develop a better classification of personality disorders. This system will probably reflect the biological factors that shape both traits and disorders. To reach this goal, we will have to learn much more about how the brain works and how individuals vary in brain function. Only then can we describe personality dimensions that truly correspond to trait variations. At present, with no consensus as to which dimensions are basic to personality pathology, we are probably best off continuing to use *DSM-IV*.

Siever and Davis (1991) have suggested the direction that future research might take. In their model of personality disorders, each diagnosis is based on a specific trait profile and each trait is related to a different set of neurochemical correlates. In this view, personality disorders would develop when the individual has an unusually high intensity of those personality traits that are most likely to become maladaptive. Although Siever's research group is actively investigating the possibility that biological markers could identify individuals at risk for personality disorders, there are no specific biological correlates of any of the present categories. Eventually, mapping the human genome might help us to predict in advance which kinds of disorder a person can develop.

ENVIRONMENTAL STRESSORS AND PERSONALITY DISORDERS

Environmental stressors do not usually elicit new behaviors. Rather, negative experiences in life tend to amplify already existing patterns. When patients are depressed, their personality traits become exaggerated; they return to baseline when the depression clears (Frances and Widiger 1985). However, even when stressors do not lead to a clinical depression, the same process of amplification can take place. Traits are most likely to become amplified when stressors are chronic and enduring (Lazarus and Folkman 1984).

How might this process affect the development of personality during childhood? Obviously, some of the most important stressors in children's lives derive from the quality of parenting they receive. The ability to raise children can be impaired if parents suffer from mental disorders, most particularly depression (Keitner and Miller 1990), substance abuse (West and Prinz 1987), or personality disorders (Paris 1993b, 1996). Traumatic experiences in childhood, such as physical abuse from parents (Malinovsky-Rummell and Hansen 1993) increase the risk for adult mental disorders. Family breakdown during childhood also makes adult psychopathology somewhat more likely (Hetherington et al. 1985).

There are also more subtle influences in the child's environment that can have long-term implications for development. As discussed in the previous chapter, effective parenting requires parents to accommodate to the individual temperaments of children, producing a good fit. When parents apply inflexible strategies, based more on their own needs than those of their children, unwanted traits in children, far from disappearing, are likely to be exaggerated.

When researchers ask patients with personality disorders about their childhood, they tend to describe high levels of family dysfunction as well as inadequate parental care (see review in Paris 1996). However, we need not attribute personality pathology to bad parenting only.

The fact is that most children survive their childhoods. It is rather striking to see how well people can overcome even the most serious disadvantages. Studies of resilient children (Garmezy and Masten 1994, Kaufman et al. 1979, Werner and Smith 1992) have demonstrated the mechanisms of this process. The most important factor is that experiences outside the family buffer the effects of dysfunction inside the family (Kaufman et al. 1979). A child who can find alternate attachments, either from a relative, a teacher, or another family, is less likely to be damaged by family dysfunction and parental failure.

The problem is that this buffering system fails to work when family dysfunction is accompanied by community dysfunction. When the social fabric is tattered, the effects of family pathology are amplified. We must consider not only family pathology but also social pathology, as a cause of personality disorders (Paris 1996). The construct of *social disintegration* helps to explain the mechanisms. This term describes a breakdown of extended family ties, a loss of social networks, a lack of community ties, a normlessness related to the loss of consensual values, and difficulties in developing and maintaining social roles (Leighton et al. 1963).

In understanding how social factors influence the development of personality disorders, we need to take into account the relationship between traits and social expectations. Some personality structures conform better than others to the demands of any particular society (Paris 1996). In traditional societies, where the norm is conformity to the larger social group, social anxiety and interpersonal dependence are more readily accepted and need not even be maladaptive. In these same societies, however, narcissistic traits that threaten group cohesion are more likely to create trouble.

On the other hand, modern societies strongly value individualism and autonomy. In these settings, traits such as social anxiety and interpersonal dependence, which interfere with independent functioning, are more likely to be maladaptive. At the same time, narcissistic traits, which tend to interfere with social networks but not with autonomous task performance, become relatively more adaptive.

In summary, multiple factors determine whether personality traits undergo amplification and lead to disorders. Some of these are biological (e.g., high trait intensity), some are psychological (e.g., family dysfunction), and others are social (e.g., breakdown of community ties).

WHY CHILDHOOD EXPERIENCES DO NOT ACCOUNT FOR THE DEVELOPMENT OF ADULT PERSONALITY DISORDERS

As clinicians, we try to understand the causes of clinical symptoms. When patients describe unhappy childhoods, we are tempted to attribute present problems to past difficulties. Do these formulations constitute truth or mythology? Even in the political and social arena, history does not always account for all the troubles in the world. In psychology, the pathways of development are highly chaotic and unpredictable.

Many personality-disordered patients have had unhappy childhoods. However, associations between risks and outcomes do not prove that one causes the other. Correlation does not prove causation.

It is also essential for therapists to understand the difference between risk factors for mental disorders and the causes of psychopathology. When we identify a risk factor, all we are saying is that its presence makes the development of a disorder statistically more likely. It remains entirely possible that most people with the risk will never develop the disorder and that most people with the disorder may never have been exposed to that risk. It is only when risk factors account for a large percentage of the outcome variance that we can even begin to think of them as causal.

One useful analogy is the relationship of risk factors to the development of heart attacks. Research suggests that coronary artery disease is more likely to develop if one has a family history of the disease, if one eats a high-fat diet, if one smokes, and, possibly, if one also has a type A personality (Slyper and Schectman 1994). However, none of these factors by itself causes heart attacks. People who are most prone to coronary artery disease are those who have several or all of the above factors.

In the same way, negative experiences in childhood do not cause mental disorders. However, when they coexist with other genetic and environmental risks, they make psychopathology more likely to develop.

Generations of therapists have taken for granted that the roots of psychological problems lie in personal history. An additional assumption is that early learning must have a greater impact than later learning, since it occurs at a time when children are more dependent on their parents and therefore more vulnerable to negative influences. Many models have assumed that the more severe the symptoms, the earlier in life must be their origin.

These ideas have not been supported by empirical research (Paris 1997a). What clinicians often fail to take into consideration is that every patient they see could be matched with other individuals who have had similar experiences, yet have not developed the same symptoms. One of the most consistent findings of developmental psychopathology is that, by and large, negative events occurring early in life do *not*, by themselves, usually lead to psychiatric disorders (Rutter 1987, 1989). Most children are surprisingly resilient to stress, but resilience can be overwhelmed when stresses continue to occur throughout childhood. Most patients who describe early traumas have also had continuous traumas.

Prospective studies of children with serious psychosocial disadvantages have consistently shown that most of them, usually about 75 percent, are resilient (Werner and Smith 1992). What determines the failure of resilience in the other 25 percent of cases? First, those who are genetically vulnerable respond more intensely to stress. Second, negative events in early childhood are associated with pathological outcomes when later negative events prevent the child from recovering from them (Rutter and Rutter 1993). In other words, negative events are not independent of each other, but linked in a cascade.

Let us consider some common clinical examples. Parental separation and loss in childhood do not lead to psychopathology in adulthood unless associated with other risk factors (Tennant 1988). Even highly traumatic events, such as sexual or physical abuse during childhood, only lead to adult symptoms in a minority of cases (Browne and Finkelhor 1986, Malinovsky-Rummell and Hansen 1993). Even multiple adversities continuously present throughout childhood do not necessarily lead to serious psychopathology (Garmezy and Masten 1994).

Resilience is another way of describing what used to be called a good constitution. Good constitutional factors include intelligence as well as genetically determined traits, such as optimism and an ability to reach out to others for support, that help individuals adapt to a difficult environment (Werner and Smith 1992). Resilience is also associated with favorable environmental circumstances. Protective factors, such as attachments to extended family or to a well-integrated social community, can buffer the effects of risk factors for psychopathology.

We must not forget how enormously complex the experience of childhood is. Positive and negative forces in the environment are in constant interaction. This complexity helps to explain why only the most consistently adverse effects can deform personality. Moreover, development has many turning points in which unexpected positive events can reverse a downhill course (Rutter 1989). Finally, development does not end in childhood or adolescence. Adult developmental theory, based on long-term prospective studies (e.g., Vaillant 1977) shows that every stage of life presents its own demands and that people continue to change in response to these challenges.

Capacities intrinsic to the individual are the best predictors of successful coping in life. Several major prospective studies have followed adolescents from different social classes throughout the life cycle (see reviews in Garmezy and Masten 1994, Vaillant 1977). These studies show that, by themselves, social adversities, such as poverty, do not necessarily prevent children from developing normally. Furthermore, the quality of childhood experience has little or no predictive value about the extent to which people achieve maturity later in life. Instead, school performance and defense styles are the best predictors of high functioning in adulthood. These findings suggest that, in the long run, constitution plays a more important role than experience in determining success in life.

In conclusion, the primacy of early experience has not been supported by empirical research. Although this hypothesis might safely be discarded, psychodynamic principles remain extremely useful for the psychotherapist. Chapter 4 will offer a different view of the role of understanding personal histories in psychotherapy.

PERSONALITY DISORDERS: A BIOPSYCHOSOCIAL MODEL

I will now summarize a theory of personality disorders that can be termed "biopsychosocial" (Engel 1980). Personality disorders emerge from interactions between biological, psychological, and social factors. Biological variability by itself determines only trait profiles and trait intensity. Psychological risks by themselves produce only short-term symptoms. Social factors by themselves are stressors with which everyone has to cope to some degree. Only a combination of all these factors would be sufficient to cause personality disorders.

Biological Risk Factors

Patients with personality disorders are more likely to have begun life with a difficult temperament. There are two mechanisms by which temperamental factors could make individuals more likely to develop personality pathology. First, temperamentally difficult children are harder for their parents to raise, and because they are more likely to come into conflict with others, they experience more negative events during their childhood (Rutter and Rutter 1993). Second, temperamentally difficult children are more likely to perceive life events as negative (Kendler 1996).

Personality traits are an amalgam of temperament and experience. However, the genetic factors in personality make traits stable. By adolescence, most people have the personality profile they will keep throughout their lives. Whatever traits we have, adaptation depends on using them flexibly. The healthiest individuals apply a range of strategies so that different situations elicit different responses. Patients with personality disorders use traits inflexibly, and their problematical behavior makes their environment more difficult.

Psychological Risk Factors

Many factors contribute to the amplification of traits. The strongest effects are derived from chronic exposure to a stressful and invalidating environment (Rutter 1989). Many overlapping stressors contribute to the same outcome, so the effects of all these factors are cumulative. The risks include parental psychopathology, poor parenting practices, family breakdown, emotional neglect, and child abuse. The more things go wrong, the more likely the child will grow into a troubled adult.

Social Risk Factors

Breakdown in the social environment is as important as family pathology in causing personality disorders (Paris 1996). The social stressors that can increase the risk that traits may develop into disorders include rapid rates of social change, loss of intergenerational continuity, lower family and community cohesion, and decreased availability of social roles.

Specificity of Personality Disorder Diagnosis

Trait profiles are the main factor determining which type of personality disorder individuals can develop. It is not possible to develop an impulsive personality disorder unless one has an impulsive temperament. Nor is it possible to develop an anxious personality disorder unless one has an anxious temperament.

The model explains why different categories of personality disorder have very similar psychosocial risk factors.

In Chapter 4, this model will be applied to psychotherapy. If personality dimensions are the main factors behind disorders, then treatment must consist of working with traits.

Before applying our etiological model to treatment, we need to understand which factors drive therapeutic change. Therefore, the next chapter will be devoted to reviewing what psychotherapy research can tell us about the treatment of personality-disordered patients.

3

Research Data on Treatment Effectiveness

Research has had rather little impact on the practice of psychotherapy. To some extent, this is understandable. Clinicians are not always interested in empirical findings with no obvious correspondence to their daily struggles with their patients. The psychotherapy research literature has had to operationalize and simplify the complex phenomena seen in practice, with the aim of measuring them precisely and quantitatively. Its results can therefore seem rather dry, especially in comparison to the richness of clinical wisdom.

Yet research has much to tell us—about therapy in general and about the treatment of the personality disorders in particular. This chapter will review findings applying to all forms of therapy and then examine studies of the therapy of patients with personality disorders. Finally, we will see what research can tell us about which patients are most likely to benefit from psychotherapy.

RESEARCH FINDINGS ABOUT PSYCHOTHERAPY

Psychotherapy Works!

Over forty years ago, Eysenck (1952) challenged psychotherapists to prove that their methods are more effective than naturalistic recovery. Seventeen years later, Eysenck (1969) remained unconvinced that any method, except for behavior therapy, could claim proven efficacy. Today, in an age when all methods of treatment are under fierce scrutiny by third-party payers, we can thank this celebrated psychologist for having laid down that gauntlet. In the last few decades, an enormous amount of research has been published that firmly demonstrates the effectiveness of psychotherapy (Lambert and Bergin 1994).

When there is a large body of data, the overall weight of evidence can be summarized using a method called *metanalysis*. Adding the findings of many research reports tends to average out many of the methodological limitations of particular studies. Moreover, metanalytic methods allow us to estimate the magnitude of treatment effects, rather than simply determine whether therapy works or not.

Some years ago, Smith and colleagues (1980) conducted a widely quoted metanalysis of the psychotherapy literature, examining hundreds of studies concerning the outcome of many forms of therapy. The review found a considerable "effect size" for the difference between treatment and no treatment. Thus, we can expect most patients to show clinically significant improvement from psychotherapeutic treatment. This finding will not come as a surprise to clinicians. As shown in a recent consumer survey (Seligman 1995), most people are satisfied with their experiences in therapy. Moreover, these measures of consumer satisfaction are supported by controlled clinical trials. In the years since the metanalysis by Smith and colleagues, many other studies (see Lambert and Bergin 1994) have affirmed the superiority of psychotherapy to no treatment. Indeed, "Psychotherapy benefits people of all ages as reliably as school educates them, medicine cures them, or business turns a profit" (Smith et al. 1980, p. 183).

All Therapies Are Equally Effective

Therapy works, but it does not seem to make much difference which method or which theory is used as a basis for treatment.

Most studies comparing dynamic, behavioral, cognitive, and client-centered therapies have failed to find that any one is more potent than the others. In reviewing this literature twenty years ago, Luborsky and colleagues (1975) wittily quoted Lewis Carroll, stating that comparative trials of therapies elicit a "Dodo bird verdict," that is, "all have won and all shall have prizes." Since Luborsky's original paper, further research (see Lambert and Bergin 1994) has consistently supported the same conclusion.

These results could be disturbing to therapists who believe that their method is the one and only way to get results. Rather, the absence of differences between procedures based on entirely different theories can help determine what is most effective in treatment. If success depends on factors common to all methods, therapy must work in a different way than many therapists think. It may not be true that our patients get better only when we make the "right" intervention. They usually improve because of non-specific factors, and these factors are only called non-specific because we do not yet know how to specify them!

The best explanation of the importance of nonspecific factors in therapy has been proposed by Frank and Frank (1991). Patients come into therapy hopeless and demoralized. When they get help, they remobilize their inner resources. This helps explain why a good relationship with a therapist is often the most important factor in the outcome of treatment. A large body of research supports this conclusion (Luborsky et al. 1988).

Interestingly, patients also say the same thing: that their relationship to the therapist was the crucial factor in their recovery. When Strupp and colleagues (1969) studied a series of psychotherapeutic treatments and asked the therapists what helped, they received explanations that tended to stress accurate technical interventions. Yet when they asked the patients what helped, few of them could remember much of the specific content of the sessions or even precisely what the therapist had said. Rather, they talked about how good it felt to be understood. Even sophisticated consumers, such as psychotherapists themselves, describe their therapies in the same way (Buckley and Karasu 1981).

The reader should keep in mind that these principles may not apply to long-term treatment. Almost all research on psychotherapy describes short-term treatments, usually extending for a few months and only occasionally going up to a year. It is possible that the mechanisms of change are different in long-term psychotherapy. Short-term therapy could depend more strongly on nonspecific factors, while specific technical interventions may be more important in longer treatments. Although we do not know for sure if this hypothesis is correct, it is compatible with research observations that personality problems require longer periods of treatment (Kopta et al. 1994). Since the most important effects of short-term therapy depend on raising morale and mobilizing resources (Frank and Frank 1991), brief courses of psychotherapy are most effective for symptoms such as depression (Elkin et al. 1989). On the other hand, modifying personality traits requires psychoeducation, a process of relearning that is bound to take time.

Interpretations Are Not the Only Interventions That Help Patients

In addition to studying the outcome of psychotherapy, researchers have also conducted studies of its process. The focus of process research concerns whether one type of intervention leads to more progress than any other.

In an extensive review, Orlinsky and colleagues (1994) examined all the research on over fifty different variables describing the process of psychotherapy in relation to its outcome. Their conclusions firmly supported the primacy of the nonspecific factors in treatment. The factors that help most in all forms of psychotherapy were: making a well-defined contract, creating a strong alliance, encouraging openness in the patient, and maintaining a focus on current life problems and relationships. The Orlinsky group has proposed a "generic model" of psychotherapy describing the common factors in all methods, from psycho-analysis to behavior therapy.

The reader should also note which interventions have not been shown to be dramatically effective in therapy. This list is rather long. It includes most of the technical methods that many of us were brought up to believe are essential for a good outcome. For example, there is little data showing that using transference or making interpretations linking the patient's present difficulties to childhood experiences yields any dramatic difference in the results of therapy.

Of course, the absence of proof does not constitute the proof of absence. Several researchers have continued to investigate the question of whether accurate interpretations lead to a better outcome in therapy. In their "box score" review of existing studies, Orlinsky and colleagues found some studies that seemed to show at least some value for interpretations, broadly defined as the therapist providing any explanation of the patient's distress. However, the results concerning psychodynamic interpretations were rather mixed. Even in those studies that showed a better outcome with interpretation, it was impossible to separate the effects of these interventions from those of the more powerful nonspecific factors.

In order to study interpretations, we have to have a way to quantify them. Luborsky and Crits-Christoph (1990) have made a serious effort to develop a method to score psychodynamic interpretations. The Core Conflict Relationship Theme Method (CCRT) uses transcripts of sessions to produce a formulation. These scores can then be used to measure the extent to which the therapist's comments focus consistently on the same theme suggested by the associations of the patient.

Luborsky and Crits-Christoph have shown that therapy had a better outcome if the therapist follows the CCRT. However, these findings do not prove that giving patients dynamic interpretations necessarily produces a better outcome. The results might also be interpreted as showing that patients are more likely to improve when therapists listen accurately to the themes they present and when therapists are consistent in following their own rules.

What looks like an effect specific to interpretation may therefore be a reflection of a good alliance. The literature consistently shows that a strong working alliance is one of the best predictors of a positive outcome in therapy (Luborsky et al. 1988, Orlinsky et al. 1994). Whether therapy will ultimately succeed is often apparent in the first few sessions, depending on the extent to which patients feel understood and on the extent to which they feel they are working well with their therapists.

On the other hand, there is little empirical evidence that focusing on transference distortions necessarily improves the therapeutic alliance (Orlinsky et al. 1994). In one striking study (Piper et al. 1991), when all therapeutic interventions were recorded, there was a reverse relationship: the more the therapist used the transference, the worse was the outcome. The researchers offered the explanation that when the alliance is shaky, therapists may, rather desperately, bombard patients with transference interpretations in an attempt to get them working again.

In summary, there is no evidence that interpretations are an essential element of psychotherapy. It remains possible that future research will succeed in demonstrating more specific effects for these interventions. However, the absence of proof, after several decades of serious attempts to find sufficient evidence, should give us pause. The next chapter will suggest a different framework to understand how psychodynamic interpretations can be useful in therapy.

Experience Does Not Necessarily Make a Difference

This finding, although quite consistent in the literature, is rather disturbing for those of us who have spent many years attempting to improve our techniques! The best-known empirical test of experience in psychotherapy is the Vanderbilt study (Strupp and Hadley 1979). The findings were that when patients were assigned either to experienced therapists or to college professors chosen for their relationship skills, both groups did equally well. However, the generalizability of this study was limited by the patient population, a well-defined but not very disturbed group of university students. Yet all other attempts to show the effects of experience have yielded only weak or unreplicated findings (Beutler et al. 1994).

My own research group (Propst et al. 1994) attempted to address the problem by applying a more stringent methodology. We examined brief dynamic therapy in a heterogeneous group of patients with depressive, anxiety, adjustment, and personality disorders. Our patients had all been preselected to be suitable for this form of treatment. They were assigned to four levels of therapists: medical students with no experience, family practice residents with limited experience, psychiatric residents with more experience, and staff psychiatrists with many years of experience. Our hypothesis was that only the most difficult patients, particularly those with personality disorders, would benefit from assignment to more experienced therapists. However, the findings were no different from previous studies. Our patients improved to the same extent, whatever their diagnosis, and no matter which therapist they saw.

Therapists obtain formal training, gain clinical experience, and read books (such as this one) about psychotherapy. Our assumption is that knowledge is power. We believe that the more deeply we understand our patients, the more we will be able to help them. The absence of effects of therapist experience seems to cast doubt on this belief. Moreover, few other characteristics of therapists are strong predictors of outcome. Characteristics of patients tell us much more about the likelihood that psychotherapy will succeed.

However, these findings do not prove that technique makes no difference at all. The evidence consistently shows that therapists who are empathic and who are good at promoting a strong therapeutic alliance produce better results (Beutler et al. 1994). To a great extent, therapeutic skill is a natural talent, although it can be taught. Again, these results point to the importance of the nonspecific factors in psychotherapy.

The conclusion that therapist factors have few strong effects on outcome may apply only to brief therapy. It is likely that in shorter courses of therapy for well-defined symptoms, nonspecific factors that raise hope in the patient are more important. In long-term psychotherapy, experience might count for more, although this remains to be demonstrated in systematic research studies.

Factors Within the Patient Are the Best Predictors of Outcome

Good patients get the most out of therapy and bad patients the least. Let us define what we mean by good and bad.

The severity of symptoms is negatively correlated with the outcome of psychotherapy (Garfield 1994). In other words, the least dysfunctional patients usually do the best. Functional level can be measured by the construct of *ego strength*, which reflects the extent to which patients can work and/or maintain interpersonal relationships. Those with high ego strength do better in therapy, whereas those who lack both a consistent work history and a history of meaningful relationships do much more poorly (Garfield 1994). Moreover, those with high ego strength are also usually more involved in psychotherapy and form a stronger therapeutic alliance.

These findings should come as no surprise to seasoned clinicians. We would like to help our seriously dysfunctional patients but, in therapy, as Horwitz (1974) once put it, "the rich get richer and the poor get poorer."

Even though ego strength is significantly related to outcome, the correlations are low (usually less than .30). Thus, there is no single patient variable that can act as a strong predictor of outcome. This is why the effects of psychotherapy, good or bad, can sometimes be surprising. As Garfield (1994) points out, even if we can predict about two-thirds of the variance in therapy outcomes by applying formal measures, that is not much better than most of us could do without such measures, simply by applying clinical intuition.

Most Symptoms Improve in Brief Courses of Therapy

There has been a discrepancy between theory and practice concerning the optimal length of psychotherapeutic treatment. Traditionally, longer treatments have tended to be seen as pure gold, while shorter ones are copper. Yet there is little empirical evidence that length of treatment actually makes a difference.

The most important research on this subject has been carried out at Northwestern University. A sample of 2400 patients followed over time was used to measure the dose-effect relationship in psychotherapy (Howard et al. 1986). On the average, 50 percent of patients show clinical improvement by eight sessions, and 75 percent by twenty-six sessions. The findings support the usefulness of briefer forms of therapy in general clinics.

Recently, the Northwestern research group has extended its findings. Some dimensions, such as self-esteem and assertiveness, can benefit from treatment of up to a year or more (Kopta et al. 1994). However, we do not have data as to whether treatments lasting much more than a year would bring any additional benefits.

The data therefore show that most psychotherapy patients do well without having to be seen for a long time. On the other hand, offering less than two months of therapy (as is sometimes mandated by managed care companies) is thoroughly irrational. For control of symptoms, therapy going beyond six months is not very cost-effective. As we will see below, however, therapy lasting more than six months is usually directed not toward symptoms but toward the modification of personality traits.

In summary, a large body of research on psychotherapy shows that psychotherapy is usually effective, but there are few differences between one therapy and another. The most important factors for outcome depend on nonspecific factors that are associated with a strong working alliance. The presence of these positive predictive factors depends more on characteristics of patients than of therapists. Most people get better in short courses of treatment. Therapy for personality pathology usually requires more time.

RESEARCH ON PSYCHOTHERAPY IN THE PERSONALITY DISORDERS

Patients with personality disorders are often thought to be refractory to psychotherapy. This reputation is not undeserved.

In studies examining the effects of comorbid personality disorders in depressed patients, those who also have a personality disorder respond more poorly to both psychopharmacology and psychotherapy (Andreoli et al. 1993, Pilkonis and Frank 1988, Shea et al. 1990, Shea et al. 1992).

There have been only a few studies examining the effectiveness of psychotherapy for the symptoms of the personality disorders themselves. The reason is that research on long-term treatment is rather expensive. Moreover, before reviewing this literature, we need to put it into the context of long-term outcome. We cannot understand the effects of treatment in any mental disorder unless we know the natural outcome of the disorder. Since chronic conditions often remit over time, a slow improvement over several years of treatment can reflect natural history rather than treatment.

There have been a few studies of the outcome of untreated personality disorders (Perry 1993). Odd cluster and anxious cluster patients show little change over time (Reich et al. 1989). By and large, improvement over time is most characteristic of the impulsive cluster. Studies of antisocial personality (Black et al. 1995) and of borderline personality (Paris 1993a) have shown marked reductions in impulsivity as patients get older. Nevertheless, in both disorders, most "recovered" patients continue to show serious personality pathology.

What is the evidence that psychotherapy can help patients

with personality disorders? The earliest study was carried out at the Menninger Clinic in the 1950s (Wallerstein 1986). The Menninger Study had many limitations: it examined only forty-two subjects, had no control group, failed to make precise diagnoses, and suffered from the limitations of measures used forty years ago. However, the findings do have some relevance for clinical practice.

The most consistent finding of the Menninger study was that patients with higher initial ego strength had the best outcome (Kernberg et al. 1972). However, there was great variability in the outcome of this cohort. Some high-functioning patients did poorly and some low-functioning patients did well. There was no evidence that using a "deeper" psychodynamic approach made a difference. Most patients benefited more from a supportive approach (Horwitz 1974). When the research group tried to predict who would do well, some interesting discrepancies emerged: higher functioning patients did poorly if they failed to form a strong alliance, whereas lower functioning patients did better than expected when they had a good therapeutic alliance. These results again point to the importance of the nonspecific aspects of therapy, even in long-term psychoanalytic treatment.

In summary, the Menninger Study was a pioneering venture, but failed to demonstrate the specific effectiveness of dynamic therapy. Moreover, the length of psychodynamic treatment had its down side: some of the patients in the study remained in treatment for the rest of their lives.

Since the Menninger study, there have been no major research projects examining long-term psychodynamic therapy in a personality-disordered population. However, several studies suggest that intermediate lengths of treatment can be symptomatically effective in some patients with personality disorders. Two reports have evaluated the efficacy of periods of psychotherapy lasting more than a year for patients with personality disorders. Stevenson and Meares (1992), examining a cohort with borderline personality, and Monsen and colleagues (1995), studying a cohort with a mixture of several categories of personality disorder, both found that patients attained clinical improvement after two years of therapy.

There are two major problems with these findings. First, neither of the cohorts had a control group for comparison, so we do not know for sure whether the improvement was more rapid than one would expect from the naturalistic effects of time alone. A study by Winston and colleagues (1994) did use a control group, and reported that in a forty-session therapy, patients with either anxious cluster disorders or histrionic personality disorder showed significantly greater improvement than did those left untreated on a waiting list.

Another problem with this research is more difficult to address. We do not know whether patients who stay in therapy are representative of personality-disordered patients as a whole. Some categories of disorder may be easier to treat than others. Borderline personality is notable for its resistance to treatment, and, as will be reviewed in Chapter 5, more than half of these patients drop out when offered open-ended treatment. Thus, those who stay in treatment are probably not representative of the larger population. What findings like these do show is that positive outcomes can be expected when personality-disordered patients are carefully selected for long-term therapy.

However, the more difficult patients have not been ignored by researchers. An important study of the psychotherapy of patients with borderline personality disorder was conducted over a one-year period by Linehan (1993). Since her findings are particular to BPD, they will be discussed in Chapter 5. At this point, however, we might emphasize that Linehan's method is the only treatment that has been shown to help reduce symptoms in patients with severe personality disorders in controlled clinical trials.

Earlier in this chapter the question of whether psychotherapy of greater length is more effective was discussed. The idea that patients with personality pathology are a sub-group needing a longer course of treatment is consistent with findings that characterological symptoms only improve after longer periods of treatment (Howard et al. 1986, Kopta et al. 1994). In another study of outpatients with personality disorders (Høglend 1993), patients with personality pathology only improved when treatments lasted for fifty sessions.

Let us examine the findings of the Northwestern University group in somewhat more detail. In their study of the relationship between treatment length and outcome, Howard and colleagues (1986) found that a more severely disturbed subgroup, which they labeled, without much diagnostic precision, *borderline-psychotic*, required a full year to show clinical improvement.

In a second report (Kopta et al. 1994), the Northwestern group broke down the dose-effect relationship according to the nature of the presenting symptoms. These findings were derived from a multi-site study of 854 patients in which patients were seen weekly in open-ended therapy. The results showed that the number of sessions needed depended on whether the patients presented acute distress, chronic distress, or characterological problems. Acute distress, such as acute anxiety or depression, improved rapidly, usually within a few months, although complete recovery could take up to a year. Chronic distress, such as chronic anxiety or depression or interpersonal sensitivity and loneliness, improved more slowly, requiring a year to obtain a significant clinical improvement in 75 percent of the cases. Characterological symptoms, such as hostility, paranoid ideas, or chronic sleep disturbances, required longer therapy. Yet in this group, only about 50 percent of cases actually showed improvement, even after a year. The symptoms in which over two years of therapy were needed to achieve improvement, at least in half the cases, included unusual levels of irritability and an inability to get close to other people.

These findings are the first in the research literature to show that long-term therapy has benefits that cannot be attained in short-term therapy. Up to now, because most patients present with Axis I symptoms, which tend to resolve early in the course of treatment, most studies have found only a weak relationship between duration and outcome (Orlinsky et al. 1994). The issues could be quite different for patients with personality disorders. These conditions, by definition, involve both chronic distress and characterological problems and should therefore require a longer period of treatment than anxiety and depression. However, the results obtained by the Northwestern group should not be used to support the idea that the therapy of personality-disordered patients has to be conducted continuously for years on end.

Having examined research on length of treatment, let us now consider the effects of frequency of sessions. Therapists coming from the psychoanalytic tradition have been taught to assume that it is better to see patients more rather than less often and tend to recommend that psychotherapy be conducted at least twice a week. Yet there has been, up to now, no empirical evidence showing that seeing patients more often makes any difference in outcome (Garfield 1994). To be fair, this question has never been adequately addressed in research and there have been hardly any well-designed studies examining therapy conducted twice a week. However, we cannot blandly assume that more is better.

In the psychoanalytic model, the purpose of seeing the patient more often is to elicit more fantasy material and to intensify the transference so as to make it accessible to interpretation. However, as discussed above, there is no empirical evidence that making transference interpretations produces a better outcome. From a practical point of view, it could make more sense to keep the focus of treatment on the patient's present life.

The next chapter will suggest a broader context for interpretations as one of several ways of demonstrating to patients that behaviors are maladaptive. It will also address the question of the optimal frequency of psychotherapy sessions. I will argue that it makes sense to see most patients with personality disorders once weekly. Doing so helps keep the focus on the management of life events and encourages the patient to learn how to cope better with relationships outside therapy.

DETERMINING TREATABILITY

A reasonably parsimonious interpretation of the current research literature is that some patients with personality disorders benefit from psychotherapy and others do not. Is there any way to separate these groups?

Functional Level

DSM-IV includes a measure of "functional level," coded on Axis V. This is a measure of ego strength, since the Axis V score depends on the capacity to work and to develop successful interpersonal relationships. As discussed above, patients with better levels of functioning before treatment usually do better after treatment.

The overall definition of a personality disorder in *DSM-IV* describes patients who have significant problems in both work and relationships. Psychotherapy, which is both work *and* a relationship, is likely to present difficulties for such individuals. On the other hand, if there are sectors outside the treatment in which the patient functions better, their existence would point to an ability to make use of a therapeutic relationship. Thus, patients who have had some success, either in work or in relationships, are more likely to benefit from psychotherapy. There is a great deal of empirical evidence that the higher the premorbid functional level, the more likely it is that therapy will be successful for a wide variety of patients (Garfield 1994, Luborsky et al. 1988) and for personality-disordered patients in long-term therapy (Kernberg et al. 1972).

Therapeutic Alliance

Every patient must form an alliance with the therapist to work toward common goals. As discussed above, researchers have developed ways to measure the therapeutic alliance and have found that these alliance measures are among the strongest predictors of the outcome of psychotherapy (Luborsky et al. 1988). However, the alliances of patients with personality disorders, particularly those in the borderline group, tend to be fragile (Frank 1992). This is one of the main reasons psychotherapy in this population is often unsuccessful.

Moreover, the therapeutic alliance can only be reliably assessed after patients have already had a few sessions of treatment. Unless we are willing to offer patients a trial of treatment before committing ourselves to an open-ended therapy, alliance measures cannot help us to decide whether to accept patients into more extensive treatment.

Defense Styles

This construct describes the normal and abnormal ways in which individuals cope with life problems. As discussed in Chapter 3, defense styles are simply another way to assess personality traits. Defenses can be assessed either through self-report inventories (Bond et al. 1983) or the scoring of vignettes from interviews (Perry and Cooper 1989). The different categories of defenses can then be ranked from most to least adaptive.

Levels of defense maturity have a significant correlation with functional levels in personality-disordered patients (Bond et al. 1983). Moreover, the most severe personality disorders, such as the borderline category, have less adaptive defenses (Bond et al. 1994, Paris et al. 1996). Measuring defense styles might therefore be a useful way of using trait profiles to separate personality-disordered patients into those with more mature defense styles, who would form stronger treatment alliances and be more likely to respond to treatment, and those with less mature defense styles, who would form weaker treatment alliances and would be less likely to respond to treatment.

Diagnostic Category

Formal diagnosis 'of a specific personality disorder can sometimes be useful in predicting which patients will respond to psychotherapy. However, measures of functional level are probably much more sensitive. The more severe personality disorders are associated with lower levels of functioning (Nakao et al. 1992, Paris et al. 1991), but there are wide individual differences in functional level among patients with the same diagnosis.

Diagnosis may be most helpful in eliminating the most untreatable groups. In the odd cluster on Axis II, schizoid, paranoid, and schizotypal personality disorders are generally unsuitable for therapy. In the impulsive group, patients with antisocial personality disorder are famously resistant to all forms of intervention (Yochelson and Samenow 1976, Gabbard and Coyne 1987).

CONCLUSIONS: CHOOSING PATIENTS FOR PSYCHOTHERAPY

In summary, the most useful measure of treatability is functional level. Work history is the most important component of functioning. The reason is fairly clear. Psychotherapy is hard work, and requires a great deal of persistence. Patients need to come regularly and apply themselves to a task. Those who have not maintained any employment for more than a few months at a time react badly to the frustrations inherent in treatment. If we exclude women working at home raising children, those who remain permanently outside the work force are a group lacking personal resources. Although no systematic study has been done of the frequency of Axis II disorders among the chronically unemployed, it would not be surprising if they have an unusually high prevalence in this population.

In order to apply our resources rationally, every patient considered for therapy needs a careful evaluation before initiating treatment. The aim would be to carry out triage among those who are untreatable, those who require primarily support and crisis intervention, and those who can benefit from more labor-intensive treatment methods. This process would allow us to focus our energies on those patients who can most benefit from psychotherapy.

Long-term treatment might be reserved for patients who have a good work history but have had consistent problems in their interpersonal relationships. Patients with long-term problems do not necessarily benefit from long-term therapy. They should not be assigned to extensive treatment simply because they are dysfunctional or because other methods have failed. Nor should we choose patients on the basis of their life histories, even if they have interesting psychodynamics. Dynamic conflicts occur in everyone and have no particular relationship to treatability. It is more rational to choose patients who are resilient, that is, those who are doing better than one would expect, given their life history.

In summary, research data does not provide reason to believe that, given enough time and sufficient skill, all patients with personality disorders are treatable in open-ended psychotherapy. It is much more likely that many patients with Axis II diagnoses, particularly those with poor work histories, will not benefit very much from psychological treatment.

What happens when psychotherapy is offered to these low-functioning personality-disordered patients? As we will discuss in Chapter 5, some of the more impulsive patients drop out, and as we will discuss in Chapter 8, patients with disorders in the anxious cluster can remain in treatment for long periods without much change.

What then should the clinician offer to personality-disordered patients who are not suited to open-ended psychotherapy? There are several alternatives. First of all, since most patients arrive in a crisis, crisis interventions provide a useful service for many. These interventions usually consist of a brief series of supportive sessions, often accompanied by pharmacological measures to relieve symptoms. Second, since many patients have recurrent crises, the ideal clinical setting for them is one where they can easily re-enter treatment when they need to. A model using multiple crisis intervention might therefore be the best way of handling the majority of patients. Finally, as Frances and colleagues (1984) have pointed out, some patients are virtually impossible to treat in therapy, and for these cases, no treatment is the treatment of choice.

Many personality-disordered patients feel better when they have a regular supportive relationship with a therapist. If we had large quantities of therapist time to dispense, we could offer some of these patients long-term supportive treatment, either in individual or group settings. However, we can safely assume that most clinicians today work in an environment in which human resources are becoming a scarce commodity. As a result, most cases are being seen in crisis or short-term interventions.

We have to use resources in a cost-effective way. Psychotherapists need to apply their hard-won skills to patients in whom major changes are possible. The rest of this book will therefore address the conduct of therapy in the treatable subgroup of patients with personality disorders.

Working with Traits
in Therapy

This chapter presents a detailed model for the psychotherapy of patients with personality disorders. It begins with a discussion of how personality traits can be used adaptively or maladaptively and then applies these ideas to working with traits in therapy. The next section describes some formal characteristics of the model: time frames, history taking, and the therapeutic alliance. The specific interventions include confronting maladaptive behaviors and developing adaptive alternatives. This chapter then describes an integration of dynamic and cognitive-behavioral methods in a two-pronged therapy. Finally, it develops a point of view on the termination of psychotherapy that is consistent with trait theory.

PERSONALITY TRAITS: ADAPTIVE AND MALADAPTIVE

Patients with personality disorders do not improve without behavioral change. Most particularly, they need to modify the maladaptive ways in which they deal with other people. Patients need not develop new behavioral repertoires from scratch. Rather, psychotherapy modifies existing traits, building on existing repertoires, and helps patients to make better use of the personalities they already have. Thus, change occurs within existing trait profiles. Breaking down character structures could end up working *against* traits, and radical personality change is not a goal for psychotherapy.

The treatment of personality disorders reverses the process by which traits originally become amplified. Traits can function at too great an intensity (as in the affective instability of borderline patients), or lead to behaviors that are applied indiscriminately to all situations (as in the procrastination of compulsive patients). When patients improve in therapy, they retain their original trait profile but at a less dysfunctional level. Even after a successful treatment, a borderline patient will still be highly emotional and a compulsive patient will still be more cautious than most.

Traits that give trouble in one context can help in another one. Returning to the broad dimensions of personality described in Chapter 1, let us describe how traits can work either for or against the interests of patients.

Extraverts who can readily meet new people, be gregarious, and attract the interest of others have an advantage in many social settings. However, extraverts can run into trouble in their intimate relationships, which do not provide a constant level of stimulation, and in which they cannot expect to remain the center of another person's attention. Similarly, introversion is adaptive in work situations that require focused attention and also helps maintain boundaries in relationships. However, introverts run the risk of failing to respond to social cues and of becoming isolated from others.

Similar principles apply to neuroticism. People who do not worry enough can be insufficiently vigilant, failing to take the necessary precautions to deal with impending difficulty. On the other hand, people who worry too much can get bogged down and lose sight of their goals. The most adaptive approach is a flexible strategy—worrying when the environment is dangerous but shutting down anxiety when the environment is safe.

We can apply similar arguments to the other three dimensions in the Five Factor Model. Openness to experience is associated with an imaginative and artistic temperament, but at some point, one faces the danger of losing grounding in reality. Agreeableness is a trait that makes people likeable, but at some point, individuals become too easily dominated by others. Conscientiousness is highly adaptive, but at some point, can shade into rigidity and obsessional doubting.

In the same way, Cloninger's four dimensions also have adaptive and maladaptive potentials. Novelty seeking at moderate levels can be associated with many useful qualities, such as curiosity and flexibility. However, when this trait is excessively intense, the individual may never settle down, flitting from one stimulating situation to another. Reward dependence at moderate levels can be associated with a useful sensitivity to other people. However, if this trait is excessively intense, one depends too much on the judgment of others, and not enough on one's own. Harm avoidance at moderate levels can be associated with a useful level of vigilance. However, if this trait is excessively intense, an individual can be paralyzed by anxiety. Finally, the dimension of persistence is double-edged. Persisting in the face of adversity is one of the most adaptive personality traits and a factor in resilience. Yet persisting too long when a situation is irremediable can also be a mistake.

Let us now consider some of the personality dimensions underlying personality disorders. Even traits that are often associated with pathology have an adaptive side.

A trend to be suspicious could put one at risk for paranoid personality disorder. Yet this trait might be useful and appropriate in a context in which other people are genuinely untrustworthy.

A trend toward impulsivity and affective instability could put one at risk for developing borderline personality disorder. Yet these same traits at a less intense level can be associated with positive personality characteristics, such as high activity and a wide emotional range. The impulsive individual needs to learn when hair-trigger responses are useful and when they are not. The highly emotional individual needs to learn when feelings are useful for communication and when they interfere with problem solving.

Inhibition in social relationships could put one at risk for avoidant and dependent personality disorders. Yet these same traits at a less intense level can produce a useful degree of caution in a novel environment. The anxious individual needs to know when a high level of vigilance is useful and when it interferes with learning skills.

In summary, the biological grounding of traits is no cause for pessimism. Personality is the framework within which therapeutic change takes place.

WORKING WITHIN TRAIT PROFILES IN THERAPY

Psychotherapy is a method of education. The course curriculum consists of showing patients how to make better and more adaptive use of their personality traits. One of the main principles of pedagogy is that learning is more effective if it takes place in a real life setting. Thus, although the "lecture" of psychotherapy takes place in the therapist's office, the "laboratory" takes place outside the sessions. Encouraging patients to learn new behaviors is the homework of psychotherapy.

Freud (1940) once called psychoanalysis an "after-education." Although psychotherapists have usually eschewed explicit educational interventions, much of what they actually do involves implicit education. Simply by deciding what to focus on in therapy, we send our patients a message. Most therapists routinely encourage their patients to try new ways of coping with problems. Personality-disordered patients, who are often locked into repetitive maladaptive behaviors, need a particularly active therapeutic technique. We need not be afraid of being teachers.

There are essentially two ways to teach patients how to work with personality traits. The first involves modifying maladaptive behaviors. The therapist helps the patient recognize when traits are being applied maladaptively and learn to apply them more judiciously and selectively to environmental challenges. In both psychodynamic and behavioral interventions, therapists work to reduce the intensity and frequency of maladaptive behaviors. Thus, in borderline personality, patients must reduce impulsive acting out and learn to tolerate emotions. In avoidant personality, patients must face the situations that make them anxious.

Some personality traits are easier to modify than others. Thus, it may be much easier to help a compulsive patient work less than to help an impulsive patient get a job. Given the intimate nature of psychotherapy, we might think of the therapeutic encounter as having an innate capacity to encourage closeness to other people. However, it may be easier to help patients who have conflicts in relationships to handle them better than to get patients who have had no relationships to develop meaningful attachments.

There is a second mechanism by which therapists can work with personality. This involves making better use of traits. Patients need to learn how to capitalize on the strong points of their characters. This usually involves selecting environments in which their traits will be particularly useful. Personality influences many choices in life, most particularly of a career. We can maximize the adaptiveness of our traits by choosing environments in which they work for us and by avoiding environments in which they work against us.

Let us consider impulsivity. Individuals with high levels of this trait might benefit from choosing an environment in which quick responses are useful. Some of the possible career choices might include joining the police force, working in a hospital emergency room, or becoming a stockbroker. Even if their occupation is irremediably predictable, impulsive people might take up sublimations, such as sky diving. At the same time, they could avoid environments in which rapid responses are a palpable handicap. For example, highly impulsive individuals would not be well suited to working in a bureaucracy.

In contrast, individuals with avoidant traits and high levels of social anxiety might benefit from maximizing predictability in their life. They might therefore want to choose occupations that reward careful, slow, and persistent work. They may also find that to the extent that they have a secure and stable social network, they suffer less from social avoidance. When their anxiety falls to manageable levels, people with avoidant traits can often be productive. To choose an example of personal significance, someone who writes books must feel comfortable working alone for long periods of time, supported and soothed by an intimate relationship with a word processor!

Highly emotional individuals benefit from working in settings where affective reactivity is useful. For instance, in occupations that involve working directly with people, a combination of emotionality and openness to experience can be associated with empathy, as well as with the effective communication skills of a "people person." Although working with other people usually requires putting one's empathy under conscious control, people who are themselves unemotional are not effective in working with the feelings of others.

In summary, when a patient is locked into maladaptive behavior patterns, we can encourage an alternative set of behaviors consonant with the basic personality. Let us briefly examine how this principle can be applied to each category of personality disorder.

Chapter 5 will describe helping borderline patients handle stormy emotions and channel their feelings into activities that increase self-esteem. Chapter 6 will focus on methods of helping narcissistic patients reduce their grandiosity and approach their goals with greater persistence. Chapter 7 describes ways of helping histrionic patients become less dependent on social reinforcements. Chapter 8 will discuss helping avoidant patients take the risks necessary to establish social bonds. Chapter 9 will describe helping compulsive patients to work without being paralyzed by doubts and perfectionism.

THE ROLE OF PSYCHODYNAMICS

The model presented in this chapter differs from traditional psychodynamic psychotherapy in how it deals with transference, interpretations, and the role of childhood experience. In each of these areas, we will reframe the classical view.

The Patient's Relationship to the Therapist

Greenson (1967) described three aspects of the psychoanalytic dyad: the real relationship, the working alliance, and the transference. A good real relationship and a strong alliance are preconditions for using the transference. However, the assumption that transference interpretations are pure gold, whereas other interventions are made of baser metals, has not been supported by research (see Chapter 3). The patient's perception of feeling understood by the therapist is a stronger predictor of outcome.

We can take the commonsensical view: patients come for help to improve their relationships with other people. A good relationship with a therapist is useful only to the extent that it provides a safe haven in which these problems can be addressed. Working issues out in the therapeutic dyad is not necessarily a sine qua non for doing so elsewhere. Instead of spotlighting the transference, we can keep the focus on strategy and tactics for adaptation to external reality. In this way, we avoid regressive complications as well as eschew taking on the impossible task of re-parenting. It can be useful at times, however, to use the transference to illustrate problematical behaviors and feelings. When we point out to patients that they are behaving toward us in the same way as they behave toward other people or toward significant figures in their past, we are simply providing examples in the here and now of problems they may have had difficulty in observing in other settings.

Interventions

Greenson (1967) developed a useful classification describing three types of interventions in psychotherapy: clarifications, confrontations, and interpretations. Greenson saw clarification and confrontation as preparatory for mutative interpretations. As described by Malan (1979), the ideal interpretation makes use of a "triangle of insight," linking the past, the present, and the transference together into one pattern. Yet, as discussed in Chapter 3, research has not supported this idea that interpretations are the crucial elements of psychotherapy.

What interpretations *can* provide is a way of showing patients why and how their behaviors are maladaptive. When we link the past with the present, what we are really telling patients is that they need not maintain anachronistic behavioral patterns. Moreover, therapists often need to redirect the patient's attention away from the past. Many patients need to avoid becoming mired in history, particularly if they use the past to avoid confronting problems in the present.

Focusing *primarily* on childhood experiences in therapy is also not consistent with what we know about the origins of personality disorders. As discussed in Chapter 2, the long-term effects of childhood depend on complex interactions between risk factors and protective factors and derive from the cumulative effect of experiences at all stages of development.

Psychodynamics remains an essential element of the therapist's armamentarium because understanding provides an *experience* of validation. This is one of the crucial nonspecific factors in therapy and is often what patients remember most about how their therapy helped them (Strupp and Fox 1969).

There are cases in which exploring the past can have more specific effects. Most clinicians have had the experience that overcoming the effects of a troubling relationship to a parent can produce remarkable changes, at least in some patients. The problem is that in so many other patients, the same explorations fail to lead to any behavioral change.

Even when pathological patterns originate in the past, it makes sense to give the greatest emphasis in treatment to those factors in the current environment that prolong and maintain maladaptive behavior. The reason therapy takes time is that it needs to examine in detail how the effects of past experience are played out in the patient's present life.

In summary, *the present is the primary concern of treatment.* Even if historical events contribute to psychopathology, understanding etiology is rarely sufficient, in and of itself, to produce psychological change.

The problem of the discrepancy between insight and action did not escape Sigmund Freud (1937). A decade later, two psychoanalysts (Alexander and French 1946) wrote a book about how easy it is for therapy to become grounded in the past and about the temptation for patients to use the past as justification for avoiding change in the present. These innovative clinicians, writing over fifty years ago, were ahead of their time. They pointed out that the structures of psychoanalytic therapy, most particularly the regularity and frequency of sessions over long periods of time, provide a haven from the vicissitudes of living that can be all too secure. More recently, Paul Wachtel (1977, 1993) has argued that insight can only be turned into action through the complex educational process that analysts call *working through*. Not surprisingly, Wachtel has been among the most persuasive advocates for combining psychoanalytic and behavioral methods into an eclectic psychotherapy.

WORKING WITH TRAITS: FORMAL CHARACTERISTICS

Time Frames

Working with traits in therapy need not involve any radical differences from usual procedures. The fifty-minute hour remains perfectly serviceable. The rules are straightforward: the patient is expected to talk about the events of the week, while the therapist is expected to offer useful comments about the course of events.

There are no solid reasons to see personality-disordered patients in therapy more than once a week. As discussed in the previous chapter, there is no empirical evidence to show that seeing patients twice a week, or more often than that, is any more effective than are weekly sessions in producing change.

There are also positive reasons for maintaining a once-a-week schedule. Therapy that concerns itself with maladaptive behavior patterns needs to deal with the events of the previous week of the patient's life.

Those who insist on the importance of frequent sessions are expressing an opinion, not a fact. In the era of managed care, we need to defend practice with solid evidence. We can tell insurers that the literature shows a value for seeing patients over a longer time. The idea that frequent sessions are necessary derives, of course, from psychoanalysis, a model of psychotherapy in which the transference is a central concern. The assumption is that the patient's relationship with the therapist must change before relationships with other people change. The idea is that personality structure must be broken down and forged anew, in what Greben (1984) has called "the crucible of the transference." The approach to therapy recommended here, however, is concerned with changing what happens *outside* therapy. For this purpose, it is sufficient if the relationship to the therapist is "good enough."

The therapy of personality disorders requires length because patients must undergo a difficult learning process. First, they must recognize that their behaviors are maladaptive. Second, they need to unlearn these behaviors. Third, they must learn new behaviors.

Long-term therapy need not mean life-long therapy. There is no clear-cut endpoint to the psychotherapeutic process. We have seen in the previous chapter that patients with personality disorders run a risk of becoming lifers. Part of the problem is that some patients are unusually needy. The other part is that their therapists keep them in treatment because they believe that longer treatment is better treatment. (One sometimes wonders whether this belief meets the needs of patients for therapy or the needs of therapists to be fully booked.) The idea that, in order to obtain substantive change, patients need to come to therapy for years on end is one of the shibboleths of the therapy literature. Yet it is not supported by evidence.

Some patients do require years to make substantive changes. However, not all long-term treatment needs to be continuous. An important but underutilized alternative is *intermittent* therapy. This idea was first introduced by Alexander and French (1946) as a way of countering the tendency of psychotherapy to be addictive or to become an end in itself.

Interestingly, therapists who have conducted long-term follow-up studies of personality-disordered patients (McGlashan 1993, Silver 1983) have often recommended intermittent treatment. Each time the patient comes for treatment "a piece of work" is accomplished. Then, in order to avoid stagnation and/or excessive dependence on the therapist, the treatment is deliberately interrupted and patients are asked to see how well they can apply in the real world what they have learned in the consulting room. After a break, they can return for another series of sessions.

Some patients naturally go through therapy in this way. Most clinicians have experienced successful treatments that were intermittent. If we are wedded to classical models, we may resist "premature" interruptions or terminations. For example, in a naturalistic study of therapy of patients with borderline personality disorder (Waldinger and Gunderson 1984), therapists perceived their patients as having broken off their treatment prematurely if they left against advice, even after they had completed several years of treatment. Yet there was no evidence that these patients fared any worse than those who left by mutual agreement. The tendency of personality-disordered patients to break off therapy might even be useful for therapists. McGlashan (1993) recommends capitalizing on the impulsivity of borderline patients by encouraging an intermittent schedule. When the patients have had enough, they can leave with the security of being able to return the next time they feel ready to work.

Content of Therapy Sessions

When we work with traits, our patients provide us with the same material as in other forms of therapy, but we use it somewhat differently.

History Taking

At the beginning of treatment, therapists obtain a complete history of the patient's personal development. These life histories place experiences in a historical context. Doing so does more than provide simple understanding. Taking into account a patient's history is *validating*. Some stories will be told for the first time. Others will be understood for the first time.

However, understanding past events is only one piece of a much larger puzzle. Although therapists highlight how present problems recapitulate past ones, they need to keep treatment firmly focused on the resolution of current difficulties.

Therapeutic Alliance

Research shows that a strong alliance is a sine qua non for the success of psychotherapy (Luborsky et al. 1988). It is particularly important for patients with personality disorders to feel the therapist is on their side, so they can hear and make use of confrontations about maladaptive behaviors. When people feel understood, they can often accept hearing what they are doing wrong.

Listening Skills and the Normative Content of a Session

As in most forms of psychotherapy, the raw material of a session should be patient-driven. A high level of listening skills is the hallmark of a well-trained therapist. Normative sessions begin with the patient's narrative, usually consisting of a report on recent problematical events, accompanied by the patient's interpretation of them. Since patients often present a one-sided story of their difficulties, it is our job to observe how traits contribute to problems. The therapist must read between the lines in order to raise questions about patients' contributions to their difficulties.

Personality-disordered patients may present narratives portraying themselves as either the victims of circumstance or of unreasonable opposition from other people. The therapist will have to counter these perceptions. One might begin by making mental notes as to how patients' versions of events can be accounted for, not by other people's personality traits but by their own. Eventually, this information will be applied to confrontations about maladaptive behavioral patterns.

In addressing a problematical situation, the therapist will need to know exactly what happened. By focusing on the details of an interaction, it is usually possible to analyze what went wrong. This resembles the method of *interpersonal therapy*, a method designed to unravel knots in relationships (Klerman and Weissman 1993).

Confrontations of Maladaptive Behaviors

In order to deal with personality pathology, patients must, at a minimum, agree that their behaviors are indeed maladaptive. The therapist must therefore confront the patient. The word *confrontation* might seem to suggest an aggressive posture. In fact, confrontations do sometimes go awry because of the way information is conveyed to the patient (Adler and Myerson 1973). It goes without saying that when we confront, we must be tactful.

In fact, much of the skill of the psychotherapist lies in being able to say hard truths in ways that people can hear. Wachtel (1993), writing about the words therapists use to get their message across, describes a number of useful ways to avoid sounding critical in therapy, including asking exploratory questions, affirming inner experience, reframing, and acknowledging strengths. Linehan (1993) similarly describes the "dialectical" relationship between validation and change in therapy. Until and unless patients feel we understand why they need to behave in the way they do, they are not likely to listen to our message about the need to change.

With all our skills, there will always be patients who, in spite of persistent and respectful interventions, will insist that they are right and that the rest of humanity is wrong. Such cases may not be treatable. Patients who are suitable for therapy will, sooner or later, agree that something has gone wrong with their interactions with other people, although they may be puzzled as to the precise nature of the problem.

Sometimes, while aiming to maintain an ideal level of empathy, we can miss opportunities to make useful confrontations. Patients may contribute to this reluctance by communicating that since everyone else has already told them their behavior is wrong, they want the therapist to provide them with support. The technical challenge is how to tell people they are wrong in a way that makes them feel the therapist is still on their side. Essentially, therapists must balance confrontation with validation.

A comparison that comes to mind is parenting. No parents in their right minds would want to remain "empathic" when children are clearly, and possibly dangerously, in the wrong. Rather, they will, clearly but kindly, confront their children about their behavior. In the broadest sense of empathy, parents show more understanding by confronting maladaptive behavior than by worrying about its roots in the child's emotional life.

In much the same way, confrontation is a crucial first step in the therapy of the personality disorders. As first suggested by

Reich (1933), unless ego-syntonic behavior can be made ego-dystonic, it cannot be addressed.

Once it is agreed that responses are maladaptive, therapist and patient can work together to establish precisely which traits are driving them. These will, in most cases, be the underlying traits behind the patient's personality disorder. For example, borderline patients react to interpersonal conflict by becoming increasingly emotionally unstable and impulsive. Narcissistic patients react with rage and entitlement. Avoidant patients respond by withdrawing. Compulsive patients react by becoming more controlling. In each case, the task of therapy is to identify these characteristic patterns.

Interpretations

Interpretations, that is, placing the patient's present maladaptive behaviors in the context of past experiences, retain a place in psychotherapy. The value of making links with the past is that they can help show patients that their behaviors are indeed maladaptive. When patients understand that they are reacting more to the past than to the present, it may be easier for them to consider alternatives.

Working with traits is therefore a two-pronged method. The first prong is psychodynamic: using interpretations to focus the patients on the process by which traits were amplified. The second prong is behavioral: reversing the process of amplification and learning new behaviors.

Development of Adaptive Behavioral Alternatives

Patients with personality disorders are locked in by their traits. Even when they admit that they are behaving maladaptively, they are often at a loss to come up with any alternatives. To deal with this problem, the therapist might ask the patient in a nondirective way, "Have you thought of how else you might have handled this?", or, somewhat more directively, "Have you considered, as an alternative, doing something like this. . . ." A number of alternatives can then be examined, with patient and therapist working together to determine their pros and cons.

Although patients often have an initial resistance to change, they want to try out new behaviors. They will usually discover that some of them are more effective than those they have used in the past. This is how patients learn to expand their behavioral repertoires.

Doing so is, of course, no simple process. The treatment of personality disorders takes time because learning is facilitated by repetition.

Wachtel (1977) points out that we need not wait for insight to develop first if changing behavior, in and of itself, creates insight. When we act differently and then discover that other people are less malevolent than we think, we realize more clearly that much of the problem has always lain within ourselves.

Personality-disordered patients have two specific problems with the learning process. First, mastering new behaviors may be difficult because of highly dysphoric emotions. Linehan (1993), writing about borderline personality, has made a number of useful suggestions to address this problem. Patients can learn to tolerate dysphoric affects either by using short-term measures, such as distraction techniques, or long-term measures, such as moving into a problem-solving mode. Teaching patients to handle their feelings more effectively is a form of psychoeducation. In patients with anxious cluster disorders, paralyzed by their dysphoria, similar principles can be applied.

Second, patients may have trouble learning new behaviors because they insist that other people need to change to accommodate them. Since this problem is particularly characteristic of narcissistic personality disorder, it will be considered at length in Chapter 6.

In summary, working with traits involves helping patients give up old behaviors and replace them with new ones as well as find new and better uses for old traits. Focusing too much on the relationship with the therapist runs the danger of providing patients a safe haven at the expense of helping them deal better with other people. To encourage social learning, therapists must focus on current life events.

Working with traits is therefore a psychoeducational model. Not all aspects of traits are genetically determined, and even those that are are still open to modification by the environment. By exposing patients to different environmental cues, present learning can compensate for failures of past learning.

A similar process takes place in normal development. Studies of children at high risk have shown that changes in the interpersonal environment can be turning points that lead to surprising levels of improvement, even among those who begin life with serious disadvantages (Rutter 1987). If such changes can happen naturalistically, then there is no reason to believe that they cannot occur in psychotherapy.

PERSONALITY TRAITS AND PSYCHOTHERAPY TERMINATION

Psychotherapy, like politics, must be the art of the possible, setting goals that can actually be met. Both therapist and patient benefit when meeting reasonable objectives makes treatment feel like a success.

If we believe that personality derives from early childhood experiences, then working through such experiences might lead to radical change. If, on the other hand, personality has strong genetic roots, then the goals of therapy should be much more limited. In this view, although personality has a structure whose ground-plan is relatively fixed, the details can be meaningfully altered.

The previous chapter concluded that we do not know to what extent psychotherapy is effective for patients with personality disorders. We need to conduct systematic research on large cohorts of patients in treatment, who would then be followed up several years after termination. Given our present state of knowledge, it makes sense for treatment goals for most patients with personality disorders to be realistic and modest. As Freud (1937) was the first to note, patients can become "interminable," and some personality-disordered patients are never able to leave treatment (Horwitz 1974, Wallerstein 1986).

Interminability reflects unrealistic expectations by therapists about what kind of change is possible in their patients. In borderline personality disorder, a large percentage of patients, even a majority, drop out of treatment (Gunderson et al. 1989, Skodol et al. 1983, Waldinger 1987). It is not entirely clear if this is a bad thing. It is possible that some patients, for reasons relevant to their psychopathology, find continuous therapy debilitating. They may be wiser than their therapists who insist on continuing the treatment. We should rarely oppose patients' wishes to drop out of therapy, as long as they can come back later.

Psychotherapy is always poised on a precarious balance point between stasis and change. Therapy has an addictive quality for some patients. Alexander and French (1946) recommended that the rhythm of treatment needs to be deliberately broken to encourage patients to practice what they have learned in the outside world.

Patients can be allowed to leave psychotherapy when they master some of their difficulties and then encouraged to return each time maladaptive behaviors give them serious trouble. In this model, we can comfortably discharge patients without having solved all their problems. There is no therapeutic nirvana. Nor is there any such thing as a complete analysis. As one should expect in a chronic illness, personality-disordered patients need to return to treatment periodically. "Retreads" are a normal outcome of psychotherapy.

SUMMARY

When we work with traits, we are helping patients understand their personality traits and make better use of them. We can capitalize on the nonspecific factors in therapy, particularly empathy and validation, in order to encourage patients to make changes in their behavior. The work of therapy focuses primarily on present difficulties, most particularly the patient's interactions with other people, which need to be examined in greatest detail.

Working with traits is an eclectic model combining the best aspects of three traditions. From the psychodynamic tradition, we learn listening skills and an ability to understand a patient's personal history. From cognitive-behavioral therapy, we learn how to identify patients' perceptions of the world as well as their skills in dealing with other people. From interpersonal therapy, we learn the importance of examining interactions with other people in sufficient detail to develop useful alternatives.

In the next five chapters, we will apply these principles to some of the most common personality disorders seen in clinical practice.

5

Borderline Personality Disorder

*Wild with rage, and resolved in revenge to bring him to
public shame at whatever cost to herself, she rushed into
the supper room, and, breaking a glass, began to gash her
naked arms with the pieces. Immediately, the place was in
tumult. . . . A few minutes later, still jabbing at herself with
a pair of scissors, she was carried from the room.*

— D. Cecil, on Lady Caroline Lamb
(mistress to Lord Byron)

THE CLINICAL FEATURES OF BPD

Borderline personality disorder (BPD) has been, and continues
to be, both a challenge and a frustration for clinicians. The
DSM-IV criteria describe impulsive symptoms (self-damaging
acts, recurrent suicidal behavior, inappropriate anger); affective
symptoms (affective instability, emptiness); interpersonal symptoms (efforts to avoid abandonment, unstable intense relationships, identity disturbance); and cognitive symptoms (transient
paranoia or dissociation).

Each of these is associated with serious clinical problems.
Impulsivity makes the therapeutic alliance fragile, and borderline patients are difficult to engage in therapy. Since borderline
patients demand immediate relief from their distress, affective

dysphoria feeds impulsivity. Since borderline patients act out when their attachments fail, unstable relationships also fuel impulsivity. The cognitive symptoms of BPD can produce disruptive micropsychotic episodes.

Clinical experiences are paralleled by research findings showing how often borderline patients fail to respond to psychotherapy. Studies of borderline patients in treatment (Gunderson et al. 1989, Skodol et al. 1983) demonstrate that when patients with BPD are offered open-ended therapy, two-thirds of them can be expected to drop out within a few months. Somewhat lower rates are seen in subpopulations preselected as suitable for long-term dynamic therapy (Stevenson and Meares 1992). The lowest drop-out rate (16 percent) has been reported in Linehan's (1993) controlled clinical trial of "dialectical behavior therapy." Linehan's method kept an unusually low-functioning group of borderline patients in therapy, and these remarkable results must either reflect the greater effectiveness of the treatment or the high motivation associated with a research setting.

Outcome studies have also demonstrated the chronicity of borderline pathology. Fifteen-year follow-ups show that, in most cases, BPD lasts for many years and only remits slowly over time (see summaries in Paris 1988, 1993a, 1994). The majority of borderline patients show some degree of clinical improvement by age 40. However, research from a variety of clinical settings documents that about 10 percent of these patients will complete suicide. Even among the 90 percent of patients who do not kill themselves, most continue to have serious interpersonal difficulties.

Clearly, we are far from understanding this complex disorder. Let us see to what extent underlying traits can account for these clinical phenomena.

THE TRAITS BEHIND BPD

Borderline pathology can be thought of as an amplification of two underlying personality dimensions: impulsivity and affective instability (Siever and Davis 1991). Although Siever and Davis hypothesized that these core dimensions of BPD have a specific neurochemical basis, this conjecture remains unproven. We can, however, hypothesize as to how borderline pathology might emerge from these traits.

The future borderline patient would begin life with an inclination to act quickly and to experience affects more intensely. When the psychosocial environment is favorable, these traits would be associated with an active and emotional personality. However, when the psychosocial environment is unfavorable, these traits would be amplified and create significant dysfunction.

What kind of unfavorable environment could be associated with borderline pathology? Research on the psychological factors in BPD has not demonstrated any single pattern. When borderline patients are asked about their childhood experiences, they tend to describe them as traumatic and neglectful. In research studies, when patients with BPD are compared with other groups, they describe higher rates of sexual abuse, physical abuse, verbal abuse, and emotional neglect (see review in Paris 1994).

In general, most patients with BPD have experienced difficult childhoods. One line of evidence supporting this view involves research on the parents of borderline patients. Several studies (reviewed in Zanarini 1993) indicate that parents share many of the problematic traits of their children, particularly impulsivity and affective instability. Thus, parents who are depressed, who abuse substances, or who also suffer from impulsive personality disorders are more likely to traumatize and/or neglect their children.

The common thread in the history of the borderline patient is a family that is disorganized, unsupportive, and hurtful. This is an environment that would be particularly likely to amplify impulsive and affectively unstable personality traits.

However, a problematical family environment is probably insufficient, in and of itself, to produce BPD. The siblings of borderline patients, who grow up in the same families, do not usually develop the disorder (Links et al. 1988). As reviewed in Chapter 2, community studies of child abuse and neglect show that most children are surprisingly resilient to stress and can grow up reasonably normal even when raised in the worst families. However, not all children are resilient. The child who develops BPD is particularly vulnerable. Thus, interactions between a pathological family environment and impulsive and affectively unstable traits lead to a high risk for BPD.

The idea that BPD is rooted in interactions between predisposition and stress was first suggested by Stone (1980). Linehan (1993) has developed a similar theory, suggesting that BPD develops only in children who are emotionally vulnerable. Unlike Siever and Davis, Linehan hypothesizes a single personality dimension, "emotional dysregulation," as the predisposing factor. In her view, this is the primary constitutional factor in BPD, with impulsivity being secondary to affective instability. However, emotional lability is also common in other personality disorders (Zweig-Frank and Paris 1995), such as those in the anxious cluster, in which patients easily become dysphoric but respond to their emotions by withdrawing instead of acting out impulsively. Thus, impulsive traits are probably necessary risk factors for borderline pathology.

Affective instability and impulsivity are linked through a positive feedback loop. As discussed above, borderline patients tend to act out when they are dysphoric and to become more dysphoric as a result of impulsive actions. (For example, borderline patients may cut their wrists when they are upset and then be upset about the wrist slash.) The task of psychotherapy is to help the patient contain impulsivity and regulate emotions.

There remain certain features of BPD that are difficult to explain through Siever and Davis's core dimensions. A surprisingly large number of borderline patients hear voices or have brief paranoid experiences (Zanarini et al. 1990). The voices they hear are usually critical, telling them that they are bad or that they should kill themselves. This quasipsychotic or "cognitive" component of BPD might derive from personality traits related to a predisposition to major psychosis. Alternatively, since borderline patients usually stop hearing voices when their mood improves, the cognitive features of BPD may derive from its depressive component.

TRIAGING PATIENTS FOR TREATMENT

We need not assume that all patients with BPD have to be offered formal psychotherapy. Usually, only a minority of borderline patients at any given time are suitable for long-term therapy. Even when they have the same diagnosis, patients are heterogeneous; we therefore need to subject every case we see to a process of triage.

Traditionally, triage refers to a division of patients into three groups: those who will recover without intervention, those who will fail to recover in spite of intervention, and an intermediate group in which intervention will make a difference. Patients with BPD who are impossible to engage in therapy may be highly impulsive and only come for help in acute situations, disappearing until the next crisis. Others may agree to take medication and be followed but show little interest in discussing their problems. How do we identify the subpopulation that can benefit from psychotherapy?

Prescribing long-term psychotherapy involves the allocation of scarce human resources. We must therefore address an ethical question: should we favor the sickest patients or should we favor the patients who are most likely to benefit from therapy? The most practical answer is that we should devote ourselves to those who can best make use of our services. Unless and until we have more effective methods of treatment, we will not be doing anyone a service by spending years in unsuccessful psychotherapy.

It therefore makes most sense to offer long-term intensive therapy only to borderline patients with high ego strength: those who can hold a steady job or attend school, those who have had some meaningful relationships, and those who have more adaptive defense styles. As Kernberg (1976) puts it, given the burden we take on in treating these patients, we might as well give ourselves a reasonable chance of success.

What then can we offer to borderline patients who are not suitable for long-term intensive psychotherapy? Many of them can be managed in multiple crisis intervention. In those clinics that work under the limitations of managed care, this is fast becoming the only option. Clinicians with greater resources may be able to offer continuous supportive therapy, either individually or in groups. This approach provides a point of contact for the chronically ill and reaches a wider range of patients (Rockland 1992). Less functional patients require less ambitious goals, and we can be well satisfied if we succeed in keeping some patients out of the hospital.

We can place the therapy of borderline patients in better perspective by examining adjunctive methods, which can be used in patients who are either suitable or unsuitable for intensive work.

ADJUNCTIVE TREATMENT METHODS IN BPD

Drugs

Today, borderline patients are quite commonly prescribed psychopharmacological agents. It is not unusual, in fact, to see them taking four or five drugs at once. The reason polypharmacy is particularly likely to be used in this population is, paradoxically, that most drugs have weak and marginal effects. Since borderline patients have strong placebo responses, pharmacology may initially seem to be effective. The greatest improvements then occur whenever the medication is changed, each time providing the patient with hope for recovery. Whenever a drug proves ineffective after a few months, another is added on. Eventually the patient is receiving a "cocktail."

Although most borderline patients are on some form of medication (usually an antidepressant), the evidence base for this practice is surprisingly slim. At best, medications take the edge off symptoms. Antidepressant drugs have a very different effect in personality disorders than they do in depression (Gunderson and Phillips 1991). Thus, when we give serotonin reuptake inhibitors to patients with melancholic depression, the results can sometimes be almost as dramatic as giving antibiotics for bacterial infections. However, these medications, when given to borderline patients, are much more like aspirin than penicillin. The patient feels less pain but the basic pathology remains unchanged. Although there is nothing wrong with pain relief, our expectations must remain low.

Earlier research, which studied tricyclic antidepressants and monoamine oxidase inhibitors in BPD, was rather discouraging (Soloff 1993). These drugs have been largely replaced by specific serotonin reuptake inhibitors (SSRIs), which have fewer side effects and are nonlethal on overdose. Thus, even when these drugs do not help very much, the patient cannot use them for suicide. It is worth noting that there have been no large-scale trials in which borderline patients have been followed for any length of time on SSRIs. Their best documented effect is that high doses often reduce the frequency of self-mutilation (Markowitz 1993).

Low-dose neuroleptics also have a mild anti-impulsive effect and are additionally useful in controlling psychotic symptoms (Paris 1994). Other drugs can produce similar results but have too many side effects. Lithium, anticonvulsants, and monoamine oxidase inhibitors are not practically useful in BPD because of their side effect profiles and because of the severe danger of lethality on overdose. Benzodiazepines are not indicated in BPD since their disinhibiting effects can make borderline patients worse (Soloff 1993).

In summary, only two categories of drugs, SSRIs and neuroleptics, reduce impulsivity and dysphoria without making the patient pay the price of serious side effects. Even the positive effects can be clinically marginal. There is no reason why BPD cannot be successfully treated without any medication. If we do not prescribe, we are not denying the borderline patient a necessary modality of treatment.

Hospitalization

Most borderline patients will have been hospitalized at some time. This does not prove that admissions are useful. Patients are most often admitted because their therapists are alarmed about suicidality. Yet hospitalization should be carried out in the interest of patients, not for the comfort of therapists. In principle, the expensive resources required for inpatient treatment should be used when there is a specific treatment plan that can only be carried out in the hospital.

A recent review (Hull et al. 1996) showed that borderline patients are most often admitted for the following reasons: (1) psychotic episodes, (2) serious suicide attempts, (3) suicidal threats, (4) self-mutilation. There is some logic in admitting patients for psychotic symptoms, since neuroleptics control these complications and hospitalization can provide specific pharmacological therapy. There is also some logic in admitting patients after life-threatening suicide attempts, at least to give us an opportunity to assess the precipitating factors associated with the attempt.

The problems arise when we admit patients for suicidal threats or for self-mutilation. Patients with BPD are *chronically* suicidal and they inevitably have acute exacerbations of their baseline level of suicidality. Admitting them every time they threaten suicide is not necessarily helpful. Moreover, we need to distinguish dangerous overdoses from wrist-cutting. Self-mutilation, one of the most characteristic behaviors seen in BPD, functions primarily as a means of regulating painful affects (Linehan 1993) and is not particularly associated with lethality (Kroll 1993). Moreover, outcome studies (Paris 1993a) suggest that BPD patients do *not* suicide in an acute crisis but at a later point, usually after multiple treatment failures. In other words, acute suicidality, however frightening, communicates distress and, paradoxically, reflects involvement in the treatment.

It may also surprise the reader to learn that there is no empirical evidence whatsoever that hospitalization prevents the completion of suicide in borderline patients (Paris 1994). To be fair, there is little evidence that admitting patients with any psychiatric diagnosis prevents suicide. The reason is that it is difficult or impossible to predict or prevent such rare events (Goldstein et al. 1991, Pokorny 1982).

Hospitalization makes much more clinical sense in suicidal patients with severe melancholic depression. In that case, we can offer specific methods of treatment for the illness, such as high dose antidepressants and electroconvulsive therapy. In borderline patients, in contrast, hospitalization often provides nothing but a suicide watch. If the patient becomes suicidal again shortly after discharge, we have accomplished little. One sometimes hears clinicians talking about admitting patients with BPD for the purpose of "safety." Yet we simply do not know whether the hospital is really a safer place for the patient.

Another rationale that has been proposed for hospitalizing borderline patients is to make it possible to carry out psychotherapy or to build a therapeutic alliance (Kernberg 1976). In recent years, managed care has vastly restricted this option. There is, in any case, no empirical evidence that psychotherapy is more effective in a hospital setting.

Some authorities believe that hospitalization actually reinforces the suicidal behaviors that therapists are trying to extinguish. Linehan (1993) discourages admission and is only willing to tolerate an overnight hold. Dawson and MacMillan (1993) take a more radical position, suggesting that we should *never* hospitalize borderline patients. They argue that admission often leads to an escalation of suicidality by reinforcing the very behavior we aim to control. The authors' view is that although one should never say never, the indications for hospitalization of borderline patients are very limited indeed.

What then should we do when the treatment is out of control and the therapist needs the help of a specialized team? In such cases, partial hospitalization in a day treatment center is probably a more useful option than full admission (Paris 1994), and its effectiveness has been empirically demonstrated (Piper et al. 1996). Day hospitals offer a highly structured program. When there are activities scheduled every hour, there is less time for patients to slash their wrists. Regression is limited by the fact that the patient only goes home at night. In the absence of evidence that full hospitalization really prevents suicide completion, and in the absence of data suggesting that these patients actually do suicide under these circumstances, it seems logical to tolerate the risk, as we do whenever we see patients in outpatient therapy.

PSYCHODYNAMIC PSYCHOTHERAPY IN BPD

Selection of Patients

Borderline personality was first defined and described by a psychoanalyst (Stern 1938). Both for Stern and for those who followed him (e.g., Hoch et al. 1962), one of the main hallmarks of borderline patients was their unsuitability for formal psychoanalytic methods. It was noted that putting these patients on a couch and asking for free associations tended to make them worse. As we have seen in relation to hospitalization, borderline patients tend to regress without a definite structure.

Over the succeeding years, two schools of thought developed among psychoanalysts about the treatment of BPD. One group recommended that most borderline patients are best maintained supportively, without trying to communicate deeper insights (Rockland 1992, Zetzel 1971). Others (e.g., Adler 1985, Gunderson and Waldinger 1987, Kernberg 1976), although acknowledging that supportive therapy is best for low-functioning patients, have recommended psychoanalytic therapy for selected cases, albeit modified by a higher level of therapist activity and structure to compensate for "ego weakness."

As pointed out by Waldinger (1987), these two schools of thought may reflect clinical experiences with different patient populations. As we saw in Chapter 3, it is not diagnosis but functional level that best predicts success in therapy. The broader population of psychotherapy patients are rarely referred to psychoanalysts. Therefore analysts may see only high-functioning borderlines who are most likely to respond, at least to some extent, to an "uncovering" approach. They may therefore conclude, incorrectly, that other patients with this pathology are equally suitable for the method. On the other hand, therapists who see a large number of low-functioning patients in a community clinic may be understandably skeptical that their borderline patients could benefit from intensive psychotherapy.

We can reconcile these views by assuming that only a minority of patients with BPD are suitable for an uncovering approach. As noted above, the fact that many vote with their feet by leaving this form of therapy indicates that it is not very suitable for the typical borderline patient.

It is also important to understand *why* so many borderline patients abandon treatment. Therapy is a slow and gradual process that might be compared to watching grass grow. The problem is that impulsive patients step on the grass! They simply cannot sit still long enough to make use of this form of treatment. Those who do stay in therapy are usually much less impulsive and more likely to benefit.

The high dropout rate of patients with BPD from long-term dynamic therapy therefore reflects a failure to select the patients who are most suitable for the procedure. It may also derive from an inflexible application of technique. Thus, many borderline patients are uncomfortable with methods that focus on interpretations of past events but fail to help them deal with current life problems.

Mechanisms of Change in Psychodynamic Therapy

Working Through the Past

The assumption behind psychoanalytically oriented therapy is that problems in the present can best be resolved when patients understand their past. The issues in the past that therapists focus on depend on the particular theory they espouse.

Some authorities on BPD (e.g., Adler 1985) believe that emotional neglect is the main problem in the childhood of the borderline patient. Logically, therapy must counteract the effects of this parental neglect by being supportive and validating. Other therapists (e.g., Herman and van der Kolk 1987) believe that traumatic experiences cause BPD. Logically, therapy must focus on uncovering and working through these experiences. Still other therapists (e.g., Kernberg 1976) believe that borderlines suffer from pathological defense mechanisms that reflect distorted internal images of self and other people. Logically, therapy must focus on the confrontation of maladaptive attitudes and behaviors, both inside and outside the treatment. The fact is, however, that none of these methods has been demonstrated to be uniquely effective.

Most psychodynamic theories assume that borderline patients suffer largely from the effects of an unhappy childhood. There are three problems with this point of view. The first is the tendency of borderline patients to blame others for their distress. It is not clear whether therapists should agree with patients who blame their families. The second problem concerns whether childhood experiences, by themselves, are sufficient to explain the development of BPD. This book has argued that the long-term sequelae of events during childhood depends on their interactions with personality traits. Even though most borderline patients have had more than their share of negative events in early life, the impact of these events is filtered through underlying personality traits. The third problem is that even when our reconstructions of the past are accurate, they may not necessarily provide a guide to what we need to do in therapy.

What role, then; should reconstruction of the past play in the therapy of BPD? As discussed in the previous chapter, the historical dimension of treatment can validate patients' feelings about the past. Linehan (1993) has suggested that validation is particularly important for borderline patients, who have often had their emotions invalidated by their parents. Second, historical reconstructions can show patients that they are responding inappropriately to present circumstances if they are reacting in a mental frame based on past experiences. However, changing these mental frames involves practicing new behaviors in the patients' current lives. As discussed in the previous chapter, we will view interpretation of the past as only one prong of a two-pronged approach to therapy.

Providing a Good Therapeutic Relationship

A great deal of change in therapy takes place through the emotional experience of being understood. As Fromm-Reichmann (1950) memorably stated, "therapy is not an explanation, but an experience." Experiential factors could be particularly important in patients with BPD.

The problem with borderline patients is that their pathology often interferes with the development of a positive relationship with the therapist. Patients with BPD may be unusually aware of other people's emotions (Frank and Hoffman 1986). Yet they have a diminished capacity to perceive other people accurately because they often misinterpret their intentions (Krohn 1974). Borderline patients tend to "split," that is, to see other people as all good or all bad (Kernberg 1976). They may therefore perceive inevitable empathic failures in therapy as reflecting malignancy or hostility on the part of the therapist.

In borderline patients, intense negative transferences can be particularly hard to manage. The underlying problem is the lack of a solid therapeutic alliance, reflecting a lack of trust in other people and a diminished capability for self-observation.

Empirical studies confirm these clinical impressions that the working alliance in BPD is often fragile (A. Frank 1992). This helps to explain why many borderline patients react badly to transference interpretations. Implying that their reaction to the therapist is based on the past and not the present can be experienced by them as invalidating. Therapists who fail to take into account the fragility of the alliance may have their blithe assumptions that borderlines *can* hear interpretations contradicted by a rageful response (Adler 1979).

Borderline patients who improve in treatment may be benefiting as much from their relationship with the therapist as from insight. Reviewing the Menninger study (see Chapter 3), Horwitz (1974) concluded that improvement in seriously disturbed patients involves a mechanism he terms "internalization of the therapeutic alliance." Adler (1985) also proposed that in BPD, patients take in the nurturing feelings of the therapist over time. In this view, providing borderline patients with a warm and supportive approach counteracts their feelings of being uncared for and being bad and unlovable. Eventually, increasing feelings of trust, developed in the safe haven of therapy, change the patient's images of self and others. Similarly, Gunderson and Waldinger (1987) argue that seeing patients through thick and thin helps them overcome their negative perceptions of the world.

These mechanisms are in accord with research findings, summarized in Chapter 3, showing that the effectiveness of psychotherapy has more to do with the quality of the therapeutic relationship than with any technical intervention. In patients with BPD who have problems relating to others, these nonspecific effects are particularly important.

Modifying Defenses

Another way to understand how therapy works in BPD is that it modifies defense styles, replacing less mature with more mature

defenses. Although Kernberg (1976, 1984) uses different terminology to describe his approach to BPD, changing the patient's
internal images of self and others is essentially equivalent to a
process of learning more mature coping styles.

How Effective Is Psychodynamic Therapy?

In spite of an enormous clinical literature, there has been
insufficient research to test the effectiveness of a psychodynamic
approach to BPD. In one uncontrolled study of dynamic psychotherapy in BPD (Stevenson and Meares 1992), patients showed
clear-cut improvement after two years, while in another (Sabo et
al. 1995), self-harm showed a significant decline within a year.
However, since neither of these studies used a comparison group,
we cannot know whether the results are specific to the treatment method.

We might wonder, nevertheless, why so many analysts and
dynamically oriented therapists like working with borderline
patients. To maintain their motivation, they must have some
degree of success.

One likely explanation is that the techniques actually used by
experienced psychotherapists are different from what they talk
about and write about. The clinician who attends a conference or
reads a book can be misled about how an expert might really
behave in a therapy session. What patients say about treatment
tends to be quite different from what therapists say they do, or
even think they do!

If we listen to people who have been treated by well-known
psychotherapists, we can get a much better idea of what actually
goes on than from their case reports. Good clinicians always do
more with patients than provide them with interpretations. The
methods that produce the most success may not be very original,
but hardly anyone has taken the trouble to describe them. The
two-pronged approach described here may correspond to how
many experienced therapists practice.

DIALECTICAL BEHAVIOR THERAPY FOR BPD

Marsha Linehan is a clinician-researcher who has, deservedly, received a great deal of attention from practicing therapists for her innovative approach to the treatment of BPD. Since it is difficult to describe this method succinctly, the summary provided here can hardly do it justice. The interested reader will benefit from reading Linehan's (1993) detailed description.

Dialectical Behavior Therapy (DBT) is an eclectic mixture of many methods. Most of its elements derive from cognitive-behavioral therapy, while others resemble psychoeducation and some interventions even resemble psychodynamic therapy. The essential elements of the model can be summarized as follows:

• BPD is a dysfunction of emotion regulation. Symptoms arise out of an interaction between a constitutional tendency toward emotional instability and an "invalidating environment," in which parents fail to help children deal with emotions. One of the main aims of treatment is therefore to help patients learn how to modulate and manage intense affects.
• The patient and the therapist must agree on the goals of therapy.
• The therapist works in a "dialectic," whereby the patient's pathology is understood and accepted, yet is still expected to change.
• Treatment targets problematical behaviors within the following hierarchy of priorities: decreasing suicidal behaviors, decreasing therapy-interfering behaviors, decreasing quality-of-life interfering behaviors, increasing behavioral skills.

These overall strategies are punctuated by a number of original tactical maneuvers. The tactics of DBT are based on the principle that people need a "coach" to change maladaptive behaviors (Swenson 1995). In this respect, Linehan's *telephone strategy* is worthy of attention. Patients are encouraged to call their therapists when they feel suicidal, yet they are not allowed to do so if they have already made a suicidal gesture! The idea is to encourage patients to call for advice about the handling of dysphoric emotions, and at the same time to discourage acting on these feelings. The telephone contact is brief and structured, and consists of instructions concerning methods ranging from distraction to asking patients to consider alternate solutions to the problems that upset them.

Unlike other methods of treatment for borderline personality, DBT has been subjected to controlled clinical trials comparing it to supportive psychotherapy in the community (Linehan 1993). The findings showed that after one year of treatment, most patients reduced their parasuicidal behaviors, were more likely to stay out of the hospital, and were generally less impulsive. These gains were retained on one-year follow-up. However, the control group tended to catch up with the DBT group to some extent at the two year point, suggesting that therapy makes recovery more rapid.

The main limitation of DBT is that the patients in Linehan's cohort did not describe feeling any less dysphoric at the end of treatment. We also do not know whether a longer course of DBT could deal successfully with the pervasive interpersonal problems of borderline patients.

It is noteworthy, however, that Linehan's research cohort consisted of chronically dysfunctional patients living on welfare. If DBT is effective in a wider range of patients than traditional psychodynamic therapy, this could be its most important advantage.

By conducting clinical trials of DBT, Linehan has challenged other psychotherapists to do the same. Her view is that the ingredients of successful therapy are not just a matter of opinion, and that if others have better ideas, they should carry out their own research. Although it is possible that the same results might be achieved using other models, they would have to be documented.

Any final appraisal of DBT will depend on conducting long-term follow-ups of treated cases. One year of treatment of any kind is not sufficient for most borderline patients. Swenson (1995) describes the results of the first phases of DBT as moving patients "from hell to misery."

Four crucial unanswered questions remain about DBT:

- To what extent are the results of DBT related to its specific techniques? It is possible that only a few of its interventions account for most of the positive outcome. It is possible that the effectiveness of DBT might be due to its highly structured program and its technical methods for developing a strong working alliance.
- Does the effectiveness of DBT depend on the enthusiasm associated with Linehan's research project, or is it generalizable to ordinary clinical settings?
- Would a longer treatment, lasting for several years, help borderline patients more? Could longer treatment address issues other than impulsivity, such as dysphoria and problems in interpersonal relations?
- Is DBT a treatment for all borderline patients, or is it best only for specific subpopulations?

Dialectical behavior therapy is the most promising recent development in the psychotherapy of the personality disorders. As Linehan has put it in a personal communication, DBT may also have succeeded in defining in a more precise way the effective nonspecific factors in psychotherapy. Similar integrative approaches to the treatment of BPD can be found in the work of Stone (1933) and Ryle (1997).

SPECIAL PROBLEMS IN THE TREATMENT OF BORDERLINE PATIENTS

There are four special problems that therapists encounter in treating borderline patients: countertransference, boundary maintenance, suicidality, and dealing with histories of childhood trauma.

Countertransference

The clinical literature on BPD (e.g., Gunderson 1984) is replete with comments as to how emotionally difficult these patients are for therapists. In a classic article, Maltsberger and Buie (1973) suggested that we can sometimes wish that chronically suicidal borderline patients would complete their suicidal threats so as to relieve us of an intolerable burden. These *countertransference* feelings led Maltsberger and Buie to suggest that if we can contain our responses to borderline pathology, treatment is more likely to succeed.

However, we should not feel badly about being upset by our borderline patients. Our responses are not unique, but usually parallel what other people feel about the patient. If a patient is inconsiderate or unfairly angry with us, we are bound to be hurt. It could be more useful to structure treatment to prevent the development of difficult situations than to spend too much time introspecting about our reactions. In this view, intense counter-reactions are a signal that we have not provided enough structure. Therapy for borderline patients must be active and driven by a clear agenda. If we try to surf on a wave of free associations, the treatment is likely to end with a wipeout.

Boundary Maintenance

Clinicians have become increasingly aware of the consequences of the failure to maintain proper therapeutic boundaries (Gutheil and Gabbard 1993). Although we have no solid data about the frequency of boundary problems in BPD, at least one experienced therapist (Gutheil 1989) suggested that sexual contact is particularly likely to occur when treating borderline pathology. Borderline patients, who so often have had masochistic relationships before entering treatment, are particularly likely to be exploited inside the treatment. Moreover, female borderline patients often have a history of having been seductive with men as a way to meet their attachment needs.

Interestingly, Gutheil's paper stimulated a storm of letters to the *American Journal of Psychiatry*, protesting that we should not blame the victim when therapists take advantage of patients. This is true, but many serious boundary violations start innocently, and only then fall down the slippery slope into sexual contact (Gutheil and Gabbard 1993). The main problem for the therapist is that borderline patients invite rescue fantasies. They are often seen, at least initially, as vulnerable and misunderstood, but lovable. This image tempts us to bend the rules to meet the patient's needs.

There are, of course, therapists who are not concerned about their patients and will exploit them whenever they are given the opportunity. Predators usually choose vulnerable prey.

Boundary violations need not always be sexual. Today, when so many therapists are women, we can see other, nonsexual ways in which boundary problems occur: physical holding, offering gifts, or making shopping trips. What all these situations have in common is that the therapist agrees to treat the patient as special. Giving in to the need to be special ends in disappointment, since the patient eventually realizes that the therapist has another and much more important life.

Suicidality

The most disturbing symptom of borderline pathology is chronic suicidality. Borderline patients can think about suicide almost constantly for years. BPD is characterized by impulsive suicidal behavior, most often involving overdoses of medication following a disappointment in a relationship. These suicidal threats are not necessarily only manipulative. They have serious long-term implications, since follow-up studies (Paris 1988) show that nearly 10 percent eventually commit suicide. The only consolation for therapists is that few of these suicides occur in the midst of therapy. As discussed earlier in the chapter, they tend to cluster in patients who are untreated or who have given up after several attempts at treatment have failed (Paris 1993a).

Borderline patients are among the most upsetting people we treat, and are usually the patients we worry about most. The treatment process can be quite stormy and there may be unpleasant surprises. Many therapists can recall borderline patients who seemed to be well engaged in therapy and then proceeded to denounce the therapist as incompetent and stalk angrily out of the office, never to come back. The harassed therapist may even end up hoping that the patient will not return.

Chronic suicidality is draining. Most therapists who have treated patients with BPD have had the experience of not knowing from one week to the next whether the patient will stay alive. To add to this burden, patients can call therapists at odd hours, disrupting their personal lives with suicidal threats.

Self-mutilation is a form of suicidality that can be particularly troubling. Cutting is, of course, one of the most characteristic symptoms of BPD. Patients may chronically slash their wrists as well as other parts of the body. Although the cuts are rarely deep, they tend to be repetitive. However, cutting is not truly suicidal behavior, and patients rarely kill themselves in this way.

Chronic self-mutilation can be better understood as a type of addictive behavior (Linehan 1993). By cutting oneself, one replaces painful emotions with a relieving flow of blood. In fact, most borderlines describe feeling better after cutting, either because their dysphoria is relieved (Linehan 1993), or because they feel less numb and depersonalized (Leibenluft et al. 1987).

Moreover, cutting is communicative. As Zanarini and Frankenburg (1994) describe, borderline patients have *emotional hypochondriasis*, that is, a communicative style that focuses on negative emotions with the aim of ensuring that others perceive their distress. Borderline patients often say that it is impossible for the therapist to understand how much they are suffering. Because they do not expect to be heard or understood, the patient has to raise the volume. Although some patients cut in secret, their behavior eventually comes to the attention of others and usually provokes a response.

Chronic suicidality goes with the territory of BPD. The therapist is therefore best advised to accept it. Moreover, therapists should not assume that they have a responsibility to prevent suicide in borderline patients. We have no evidence whatsoever that we know how to prevent patients from completing suicide. Furthermore, attempting to do so, particularly by repeatedly hospitalizing them, runs the risk of making them worse.

Ultimately, therapy is about helping patients solve problems. If we spend all our time worrying about suicide, therapy becomes derailed. We need to keep our focus on the task at hand and to understand suicide threats as communications of distress.

What this means in practice is that therapists need to have thick skins. We need to let patients know that we hear them and that we are aware of their suffering, yet we need to get on with the tasks of therapy. Even though maintaining one's sangfroid in the face of blood-curdling threats is easier said than done, it is the only way to make progress.

Therapists writing about BPD have offered many different suggestions for how to deal with suicidality. These range from making explicit contracts with the patient to control suicide threats (Yeomans et al. 1992) to deliberately focusing on suicidality in order to extinguish it (Linehan 1993). We do not really know what the best approach is or whether different patients need different approaches. The proposals in this chapter integrate the author's experience with some useful ideas from the clinical literature.

A therapist working with a borderline patient must first listen to the emotional content of suicidality and validate the feelings behind the patient's despair. The second step is focusing on the reasons the patient feels suicidal. The third step is to dialogue with the patient about developing alternative solutions to problems.

When therapy is beginning to be successful, we often find that suicidality drops out of the clinical picture. The explanation is a matter of common sense: when patients feel empowered by mastery of problems, they have no good reason to consider suicide.

Borderline patients remain suicidal for long periods of time because they do not feel in control of their lives and actually *need* to be suicidal (Fine and Sansone 1990). If one has no power over life, one can still have the power to choose death. From this point of view, we should be cautious about removing a useful coping mechanism. For some patients, only the knowledge that they can die allows them to go on living.

Histories of Childhood Trauma

In the last ten years, researchers and clinicians have become interested in reports of traumatic experiences during childhood in borderline patients. As discussed earlier in the chapter, a fairly large body of research (summarized in Paris 1994) shows that patients with BPD describe experiences of childhood sexual and physical abuse more frequently than do patients with other psychiatric disorders. These observations have led some therapists (e.g., Herman and van der Kolk 1987) to conclude that borderline pathology is caused by traumatic experiences, and that BPD might better be classified as a chronic form of posttraumatic stress disorder. These ideas have become current among those therapists who are keen to search for memories of childhood trauma in their patients. However, the conclusion that borderline pathology is a form of PTSD is premature and unjustified. Let us examine the reasons for this assessment.

First, the fact that borderline patients report these experiences does not prove that they are the *cause* of their psychopathology. Correlation does not prove causation, and trauma and BPD might be correlated because both are associated with a less apparent third factor. In the case of BPD, this latent variable could be family dysfunction, which is known to be strongly associated with both childhood traumatic experiences and the impulsive personality traits that make it more likely that a child will be traumatized.

Second, a different picture of the effects of sexual and physical abuse emerges when we move from the clinic to the community. Studies of abused children in the general population (Browne and Finkelhor 1986, Malinovsky-Rummell and Hansen 1992) show that abuse experiences do not necessarily cause mental disorders and do not even lead to consistent long-term sequelae. In general, just about a quarter of abused children have measurable levels of psychopathology. Only the most severe abuse has a high risk of being pathogenic, and even in these cases, the majority of children are resilient.

Third, we cannot know if the memories reported by borderline patients are always accurate. Patients with BPD are known for their tendency to distort history, usually in a negative direction. When therapists press them for memories of abuse, they are often suggestible. Finally, as supported by a wide body of research (Paris 1995), "recovered memories" are highly unreliable, often reflecting the result of overzealous suggestions from therapists. The most reliable memories of abuse are probably those that have always been present in the patient's mind, but were suppressed rather than repressed (Paris 1995).

The important point for the therapist to keep in mind is that borderline personality disorder has not one, but many causes. BPD is best understood multidimensionally. Borderline patients cannot be understood as suffering from posttraumatic stress disorder because most children exposed to trauma never become borderline and because the majority of borderline patients lack a history of severe trauma (Paris 1994).

In summary, the etiological factors in BPD are complex and biopsychosocial. The biological risks involve an abnormal temperament (Siever and Davis 1991). The psychological risk factors include the effects of parental pathology, trauma, parental neglect, and family dysfunction (Paris 1994). In adult life, BPD symptoms can remain dormant until precipitated by negative life events (Labonté and Paris 1993). Finally, there are important social factors in BPD, since social breakdown deprives young people of structures that support identity formation and the development of interpersonal networks (Millon and Davis 1995, Paris 1996).

This model of BPD has important clinical implications. When we work with borderline patients, we should not seek simple explanations for their pathology. We certainly need to listen to patients when they describe childhood trauma and to understand how such experiences may affect adult functioning. However, therapy in borderline personality disorder need not follow the game of "find the traumatic experience." The impact of trauma can only be understood in interaction with many other factors.

Yet, theories of trauma are tempting, probably because they are so dramatic. Traumatic events have been always well-beloved in novels and cinematic portrayals of mental illness. The Hollywood model of psychopathology, in which patients are cured when they remember a traumatic experience, continues to have a great appeal.

In those borderline cases (about one-third) where there are significant traumatic childhood histories, the therapist must help patients deal with those experiences. Doing so provides a good example of the importance of validation in psychotherapy. In most cases, it is therapeutic to tell the story to a disinterested observer who validates the historical facts and acknowledges that something bad happened to the patient. It can also be important to acknowledge that the patient's family may have been inadequate in helping the child overcome a traumatic experience.

STARTING THERAPY: ALLIANCE AND STRUCTURE

The first step in any psychotherapy usually involves building a strong alliance. Since therapeutic alliances in borderline patients are famously fragile, unless the early stages of treatment are devoted to promoting the working alliance, the patient is likely to leave.

There are two elements in this process. The first is providing sufficient emotional support to create a holding environment. This means providing enough empathy for borderline patients to work in therapy. The second element is encouraging the patient to self-observe. This can be a difficult task in patients who alternate between victimization and self-hatred. However, if patients feel that the therapist is on their side and that their inner worlds are validated, they may, gradually, accept clarifications and confrontations about behavioral problems.

The therapeutic alliance is built around a structure. Borderline patients have a strong need for predictable expectations, no matter how much they test boundaries. Therefore the session should usually be at the same time every week and be of the same length. (We should all know from experience that rescheduling a session with a borderline patient is asking for trouble.)

Since borderlines suffer intensely, many clinicians have assumed that they must be treated intensely. It is tempting to believe that seeing a patient twice or three times per week makes treatment more efficient. Unfortunately, there is no evidence that this is the case. We also have a good deal of clinical experience suggesting that frequent sessions can be regressive. Until we have evidence to the contrary, it seems safest to offer most patients once weekly sessions.

In any case, most of the work of therapy has to be done by the patient, who must learn to problem solve outside the treatment sessions. We cannot, in any case, meet the attachment needs of our patients, nor is it is possible to re-parent them. We need not feel guilty about not giving patients all the time they ask for.

WORKING WITH IMPULSIVITY

The overall principles for the management of impulsivity in BPD are: understanding the communicative functions of impulsivity, helping patients identify the emotions behind their actions, and encouraging patients to learn alternative ways of handling these emotions.

We can illustrate these principles by examining some of the most common impulsive behaviors seen in borderline patients.

The threat of suicide in BPD is a source of anxiety for most psychotherapists. Yet, if we understand the meaning of suicidality, it makes sense not to respond directly to threats. Suicidality has to be tolerated because it is the patient's way of expressing distress. The therapist should therefore respond to suicidal thoughts and behaviors as communications to be understood rather than threats to be acted on.

For example, when patients slash their wrists, the therapist should spend more time talking about their level of distress and less time talking about the slashed wrist. Similarly, after an overdose of pills, although patients sometimes have to be treated medically, we should quickly resume the tasks of therapy and explore the circumstances leading up to the suicide attempt.

This does not in any way imply that therapists should ignore suicidal behaviors. On the contrary, we need to hear what the patient is trying to say. The point is that suicide must not dominate the agenda of therapy. The treatment will be derailed if we expend all our energies trying to put out fires and fail to focus on the problems that make the patient suicidal in the first place. Moreover, concentrating on saving patients from suicide can lead to therapist burnout. Most of us have probably seen examples of this sequence in which the therapist becomes exhausted and eventually abandons the patient.

In summary, suicidal behaviors should be addressed by moving to a problem-solving mode. By doing so, therapists communicate that they are not paralyzed with anxiety by the patient's suicidality and that they are interested in *why* the patient feels suicidal.

Borderline patients show a wide range of other impulsive actions. They may abuse substances, be sexually promiscuous, or have tantrums in which they destroy property. In each of these situations, the behavior might be understood as *acting out*, an action defense that functions to suppress painful emotions. The task of the therapist, therefore, is to work with patients to help them identify these underlying emotions and to examine in what alternative ways they might have handled their dysphoria.

Impulsivity in BPD involves a range of behaviors that, like suicidality, function to relieve dysphoria, and behaviors that interfere with the process of therapy itself. These "therapy-interfering behaviors" (Linehan 1993) can occur either inside or outside the treatment setting. Some of them, such as severe substance abuse, may have to be controlled before any substantive therapy can take place. Other common behaviors that interfere with therapy include missing sessions entirely and/or refusing to take responsibility for doing so. Some patients may "act in," even to the point of screaming or breaking things during therapy sessions. At some level of impulsivity, therapy becomes impossible. The patient needs to know there are limits beyond which treatment may have to be discontinued.

WORKING WITH AFFECTIVE INSTABILITY

The general principles for modifying affective instability are: tolerating intense emotions, teaching patients how to tolerate negative emotions, and teaching patients how to deal with the problems behind their emotions.

Borderline patients have stormy lives. They often feel themselves blown about by a hurricane of emotions. Buffeted by these intense affects, therapists can feel the same way, and they may find themselves dividing their week into the days they see borderline patients and the days when they do not. These reactions demonstrate that strong emotions are highly contagious. The therapist treating BPD must therefore be adequately self-protective. The antidote to excessive emotionality is, ultimately, "sweet reason." Isolation of affect is a useful defense when emotions are strong, and a therapist who is not also prone to be emotionally labile may be better at treating this population.

At the same time, therapists working with borderline patients must be highly skilled in empathy. We need to understand extremely dysphoric emotions, even when they are far from our own experience. There are many times in treatment when patients are suicidal because they are seeking an escape—any escape—from feelings. Accepting and working with emotions provides an implicit holding environment for the patient. Often, more active work on problem-solving may have to be put on hold until intense feelings are processed.

Inability to control anger is one of the diagnostic criteria for BPD. The problem for therapists is that anger is often directed at us. It is very distressing, particularly after having worked hard to empathize with a patient, to be told that one is uncaring, incompetent, or both. In these circumstances, it takes all one's experience and skill to stand back and realize a simple fact: *this is what it is like to treat a borderline patient.*

Anger is not the only emotion that troubles patients with BPD. More often, the patient is chronically depressed and anxious. It is particularly difficult for therapists to shield themselves from the patient's hopelessness, albeit necessary for protection against hating the patient for making us feel like bad therapists (Maltsberger and Buie 1973).

Finally, therapists have to be careful about their positive emotions. Borderline patients are particularly likely to fall in love with their therapists and to either allow or encourage boundary violations (Gutheil 1989). On a more benign level, there are days when these patients make us feel like deeply caring and brilliantly insightful professionals. The crash that inevitably ensues at the next session can be all the more hurtful if we have accepted these idealizations.

Teaching Patients to Manage Negative Emotions

Helping borderline patients manage dysphoria is a central element of treatment. Dialectical behavior therapy focuses on this issue and offers many creative suggestions about emotion management, which the reader might wish to consult (Linehan 1993). Most people benefit from distraction. Most people also find that a positively reinforcing activity will buffer negative feelings. However, all patients have to learn on an individual basis what works when they are upset. The crucial point for borderline patients is to learn that there are ways other than impulsive actions to relieve dysphoria.

Solving the Problems That Produce Negative Emotions

Borderline patients often feel incapable of dealing with the real issues in their lives. This is precisely why they act out to relieve dysphoria. They must therefore be brought from an emotion-driven mode into a problem-solving mode.

In focusing on the problematic impulsivity and emotionality of borderline patients, we should not forget how important it is for them to function well in at least some sector of their lives. Patients with BPD need, above all, to develop *competence* (Kroll 1988). If they attain competence, then they can retain stable sources of self-esteem outside the arenas of conflict (McGlashan 1993), whatever the difficulties they have in their intimate lives.

As discussed in Chapter 4, psychotherapy in the personality disorders focuses on problems in current interpersonal relationships. In BPD, these conflicts may appear at school or on the job. Often, teachers, supervisors, or colleagues are seen as uncaring or abusive. These perceptions may have a grain of truth, but they are filtered through the cognitive schema of the patient, who sees the world as made up of people who are either loving or totally untrustworthy. The therapist helps the borderline patient to see others ambivalently and to negotiate conflicts rather than feel victimized.

Most of the work with borderline patients involves dealing with more intimate relationships—with lovers, with close friends, and with family members. Borderline patients are quick to move close to other people and quick to become disappointed with them. This pattern, once identified, can be changed by teaching patients to slow down emotionally when they meet new people, and take the time necessary to assess their good and bad qualities. Borderline patients have to learn eventually to absorb the inevitable disappointments associated with every human relationship.

This process might also be thought of as modifying a maladaptive defensive style: splitting. Over time, patients replace splitting with the ambivalence that characterizes all mature relationships. Instead of seeing a person as all good on Monday and all bad on Tuesday, the patient learns that on any given day, people have good and bad qualities.

REASONABLE AND UNREASONABLE EXPECTATIONS IN BPD

As we work with borderline patients, we should keep in mind that we do not really expect all of their problems to be solved during therapy. Unreasonable expectations can make the treatment interminable, and when therapy becomes interminable, patients can feel they have failed. (This could be still another explanation for why large numbers of borderline patients leave long-term treatment against advice.) On the other hand, breaking off therapy after some degree of improvement can give the patient a feeling of accomplishment, which can then contribute to the alliance when the patient returns to treatment.

In a course of psychotherapy, borderline patients must learn to control their impulsivity and affective instability, and to improve their work competence and their capacity to manage interpersonal relationships. Although this progress will usually be incomplete and fragile, it may be useful to interrupt the treatment once there is a palpable improvement, and leave the door open for the patient to return later.

We should place the treatment of a chronic disorder in the context of studies of its long-term outcome (Paris 1993a). Any results in therapy have to be measured against the natural course of the illness. In the short term, by and large, borderline patients are, in Schmideberg's (1959) memorable phrase, "stably unstable." Although some degree of improvement can occur within the first few years (Najavits et al. 1995), most cases have a smoldering and intermittently symptomatic course.

Fifteen years after their first presentation, borderline patients show more stable levels of improvement (Paris 1993a). However, only a minority of cases recover completely. More frequently, patients get better over time but are unable to achieve lasting intimate relationships and are less likely to have children (Stone 1990). Stable improvement can therefore be associated with a greater investment in career and the development of competence (McGlashan 1993), accompanied by some degree of withdrawal from intimacy (Paris et al. 1987). These outcomes should not be considered, either by the therapist or the patient, to be failures. Many patients who do not tolerate a close relationship can be helped to live alone and find satisfactions in life other than starting their own families.

We cannot know how high a level of functioning any particular borderline patient will attain. Realistic expectations consist of helping borderline patients manage impulsivity and affective instability. As the outcome literature shows (Paris 1994), those who have borderline personality disorder in youth remain vulnerable to continued difficulties later in life. Therefore, most borderline patients will need to have intermittent treatment involving access to further therapy at subsequent points in their life cycle.

CASE EXAMPLE 1: MIRA

History

Mira was a 25-year-old graduate student who presented for therapy because of suicidal ideas and self-mutilation. Mira also complained of voices in her head telling her to kill herself. She was having great difficulty completing her work at school as well as problems in a love affair with a fellow student.

Mira came from an East Indian family and described her

parents as well-meaning but insensitive. They had immigrated to Canada in their twenties and worked hard to achieve success. They had also expected their children to be brilliant and perfect. The older brother, who had become a professional, fully met these expectations. Mira, who did not, was the black sheep.

Mira had upset her parents by taking on many of the accoutrements of a North American adolescence. She wrote poetry, dressed as a bohemian, and wore her hair in a punk style. Unbeknownst to her parents, she also became sexually promiscuous and abused alcohol and hashish.

Mira was rescued, at least in the short run, from these difficulties when she fell in love. Kush and Mira, who shared strong commitments in politics and literature, became inseparable. Although he was Sikh while she was Hindu, her family accepted him.

In this relationship, Kush, who had grown up in a much more supportive family, functioned as the caretaker. When Mira refused to get out of bed and go to class, he would bring her the notes. When she could not get her work in on time, he would type her papers on the computer. In the early stages of their relationship, Kush saw Mira as a beautiful and talented woman he could rescue. Over time, he felt more and more burdened by her needs. He wanted to leave her but could not muster the courage to do so.

Mira's strong needs were related to her perception of her parents as having had a limited capacity for empathy with children's feelings. For Mira's brother, this deficiency had not led to psychopathology. However, Mira's personality traits, particularly her affective instability, made her feel that being misunderstood was devastating. She therefore sought understanding elsewhere, at last finding her soul mate in Kush. The problem was that the more Kush tried to please her by acceding to her demands, the more she needed. Kush would then feel guilty and try even harder to please. The result was an impasse.

Kush was particularly upset by Mira's wrist cutting, which

was her usual way of dealing with severe frustration. Mira had begun to self-mutilate in her adolescence. Initially this behavior functioned to communicate her resentment against the insensitivity of her family. On one notable occasion, while her parents entertained guests for dinner, she came down the stairs dripping blood from numerous cuts on her arms. On another occasion, her parents found her in her room with blood-soaked bedsheets. Mira had composed a suicide note written in her own blood, stating, "This is your daughter."

More recently, Mira's self-mutilation was linked with her jealousy. Kush, who was a good-looking man, was faithful but far from indifferent to the attentions of flirtatious women. On two separate occasions, after the couple had attended a party, they quarreled over the time Kush spent with another female. Fueled by her excessive alcohol intake, these evenings ended with Mira breaking a number of items in their apartment as well as slashing her wrists.

Therapy

Suitability for Treatment

There were a number of signs that therapy could be helpful for Mira. In spite of her florid symptomatology, she had maintained a high functional level and was always able to manage her studies. Moreover, Mira had maintained, however conflictually, a long-term intimate relationship with a man.

Alliance and Structure

The initial stages of treatment concentrated on alliance building. Mira kept an ironic distance from the therapist as she had with other authority figures in her life. Yet in spite of her impulsivity, she was never in danger of abandoning therapy.

Simply providing a holding environment brought many of Mira's symptoms under control. The most dramatic features of her disorder, self-mutilation and hallucinations, disappeared when she had been coming steadily for about a month. The next task was to address the underlying maladaptive patterns of which these symptoms were the manifestation.

Modifying Impulsivity and Affective Instability

Confrontations of Maladaptive Behaviors

Mira had hair-trigger responses to perceived disappointments and rejections. The therapist was careful to validate these reactions as understandable, but pointed out that many of the situations that disturbed her could be seen by other people as relatively benign. For example, when either her boyfriend or her thesis supervisor was preoccupied with other matters, Mira felt afraid of being completely abandoned. As a result, she would go into a tailspin and think about cutting herself. The therapist encouraged her to see these reactions as exaggerated and to reframe situations in which her difficulties were not the central concern of other people.

The Psychodynamic Prong: Examining the Historical Context

The therapist offered one major psychodynamic interpretation: that Mira's experiences in her family had made her unusually sensitive to feeling misunderstood and rejected. She tended to generalize these experiences, responding to the situations that seemed to re-evoke them. The goal of these interpretations was to place Mira's reactions to other people in a historical perspective and to allow her to see how maladaptive they were.

The Behavioral Prong: Development of Adaptive Alternatives

Mira's impulsivity and affective instability reinforced each other, creating a positive feedback loop that could easily run out of control. In view of her difficulty in controlling her responses to threatened abandonment, much of the therapeutic work consisted of examining incidents that evoked these feelings when they occurred.

Each time Mira was tempted to cut her wrists, the therapist would encourage her to examine the feelings leading to the impulse and then to consider alternative ways of handling these emotions. Thus, she was encouraged to identify her responses at an early stage so that she could learn to process them internally. For example, if she could voice her feelings of disappointment about feeling neglected by Kush, she was less likely to act them out in a dramatic way. By expressing her emotions without having to turn up the volume, she found she was actually more likely to be heard.

Nonetheless, the attachment to Kush had long since passed a breaking point. When Mira stopped blackmailing him, he felt liberated from guilt and indicated he was ready to end the relationship. Within six months of the beginning of therapy, they decided to part amicably. Paradoxically, Mira felt better after this decision. The relationship had long since failed to provide her with any sense of worth. After the breakup, Mira began to build a wider social network among her fellow students. She concentrated on her master's thesis, which provided her with a more stable form of self-esteem. Mira accepted that she would have to avoid intimate heterosexual relationships for some time, at least until she was on her feet.

Making Better Use of Existing Traits

Mira's intense emotionality had to be modulated, but could also be sublimated. Thus, she used her talent as a poet to express many of the feelings that overwhelmed her. The process of writing imposed a useful structure and discipline on her affective experiences. Even if the source of a poem was intense emotion, it was buffered by the craft of words.

Mira's affective lability had also made her a passionate advocate of political causes. She used this more effectively by becoming active in her graduate students' association. Mira could argue long into the night with her friends about political and social issues. She was never in danger of becoming dull.

Outcome

Mira left therapy when she was accepted to a Ph.D. program nearer her home. As she anticipated the end of the treatment, her hallucinations returned. However, the pattern seen at the beginning of her treatment repeated itself: as soon as she connected with a new therapist, all psychotic symptoms disappeared.

On five-year follow-up, Mira was functioning much better. She was still being followed supportively, albeit intermittently, by the therapist to whom she had been transferred. She no longer self-mutilated and her hallucinations were controlled without medication. In the interim, she had, to the distress of her family, married a man of Anglo-Saxon background. Since this relationship was reasonably successful and since she had not been able to organize herself sufficiently to write a Ph.D. thesis, she abandoned graduate school. Mira was now living with a protective husband, devoting herself to writing poetry.

CASE EXAMPLE 2: SYLVIE

History

Sylvie was a 22-year-old special education teacher who was assessed following a brief admission to the hospital. She had become suicidal after a visit to her father in Europe. She also complained of auditory hallucinations, symptoms that had been troubling her on and off for several years. In addition, Sylvie reported chronic mood swings varying from feeling nothing at all to feeling suicidal depending on what happened during the course of the day.

Sylvie was the older of two daughters. Her parents were chronically estranged and unable to attend to her emotional needs. A serious trauma was inflicted on her when a male friend of the family molested her when she was 9 years old. Although she did tell her parents, they took no action other than to keep her away from the perpetrator. This incident demonstrated to Sylvie that she could not count on her family. A year later, her mother left the family to live with a lover; she only took the children back the following year when the father moved to Europe for business reasons.

As an adolescent, Sylvie learned one sure method of obtaining the attention she lacked at home. Boys saw her as lively and sexy and she found that she got a kick out of seducing as many of them as possible. This became an ingrained pattern over the years, so much so that her friends described her behavior by quipping, "the moose is on the loose."

At the age of 19, she met Yves, who became the most important man in her life. Yves was supportive of her, forgave her infidelities, and even accepted her "spells." These consisted of dissociative states in which she would break into uncontrollable crying for hours at a time and then begin to hear voices, appearing to be out of contact with her environment. During one of these spells, she actually set herself on fire, but was rescued by Yves before being injured.

In spite of the relative stability of this relationship, Sylvie was frightened of intimacy. After the couple finally moved in together, Sylvie had a series of serious spells, and then proceeded to go back on the hunt. In the early months of the treatment she became involved with a co-worker. John, who was already living with a woman about whom he was ambivalent, had no interest in a long-term relationship. As a result, Sylvie could enjoy the excitement of their secret affair, which mostly involved meeting at his apartment and spending the afternoon having sex.

Therapy

Suitability for Treatment

Like Mira, Sylvie, in spite of severe symptoms, was able to work steadily at her job and had been able to maintain a long-term relationship with a man. These strengths pointed to her capacity to benefit from psychotherapy.

Alliance and Structure

The initial sessions concentrated on building an alliance, largely by validating Sylvie's emotions. In view of Sylvie's history of impulsivity, the therapist also emphasized the importance of regular attendance. Sylvie had been given pharmacological agents in the hospital. Neuroleptics were useful in helping her to stop hearing voices, but she failed to show any clear-cut response to a serotonin reuptake inhibitor. At Sylvie's request, all regular medications were discontinued after two months, after which she used a low-dose neuroleptic on an intermittent basis to abort her spells.

Modifying Impulsivity and Affective Instability

Confrontations of Maladaptive Behaviors

Sylvie usually suppressed her emotions to the point that she was unaware of them. When she felt angry, either at work or at home with Yves, she would usually shrug off the feeling with a humorous quip. Eventually her inner feelings would build to the point of eruption, leading either to impulsive actions or to spells.

In spite of his high level of tolerance, Sylvie experienced Yves as an uncaring parental figure. She would demand constant displays of affection, which Yves found rather tiring. At these times, Sylvie would turn to John, who made her feel important and desirable.

The Psychodynamic Prong: Examining the Historical Context

The main dynamic formulation offered to Sylvie concerned the reasons why she had never learned to understand or to control her feelings. Emotions had never been validated in her family, most particularly when the parents were too preoccupied with their marital issues. This was less of a problem for Sylvie's younger sister, who had more compulsive traits and became a successful lawyer, than for Sylvie, whose affective responses were more intense and could not be continuously suppressed or sublimated. When she reached adolescence, she began to develop overt impulsivity. In her current relationship with Yves, she had come to experience a sense of neglect in the same way, and acted out in the same way as she had done before.

Sylvie took one practical step as a result of understanding her history. Early in her therapy, she took action to redress a traumatic incident from her childhood, bringing a civil suit against the perpetrator. The man admitted his offense and the court made a judgment in her favor. Although no money changed hands, Sylvie felt empowered and validated by this process. The complaint about her molestation was an example of others she might have made, particularly against her family, but Sylvie had no wish to endanger the links she now enjoyed with her parents.

The Behavioral Prong: Development of Adaptive Alternatives

The therapist emphasized that Sylvie needed to become aware of her feelings at an earlier stage. Only then could she have any chance to break the cycle and consider other, more adaptive alternatives. Sylvie therefore learned to pay attention to her inner feelings on a daily basis. It was a small triumph, for example, for her to cry appropriately in therapy when talking about difficult issues, and, instead of having a spell, to pull herself together afterwards. Practicing these skills helped her to avoid having uncontrollable affective storms that could progress to the point where she would hear voices telling her to kill herself.

Therapy offered a holding environment that buffered Sylvie against affective instability. At the same time, the therapist encouraged Sylvie to observe those events that would be expected to upset her and to be highly suspicious of herself when she seemed to have no emotional reaction at all. The principle was to open the valve before the pressure of emotions reached explosive proportions. As she did so, Sylvie had less need to act out through sexual promiscuity and the spells became more infrequent.

Making Better Use of Existing Traits

Sylvie's impulsivity and affective lability, however much they created problems, had a potentially positive side. She was an active and lively woman with a good sense of humor. When these traits became less exaggerated, they began to work for her. People often took to Sylvie, so she never lacked for friends or for a new job. Although she learned to control her self-destructive impulses, she remained action-oriented. Although she learned to modulate her emotionality, she remained appealingly emotional.

Outcome

Sylvie continued living with Yves but remained unsure whether the relationship had a long-term future. To build up her self-esteem, she concentrated more of her energies on her work and took a new job teaching the retarded. Sylvie's charm and vivaciousness, instead of being used to seduce men, could be applied to helping troubled children.

Over the next two years, Sylvie was in and out of therapy several times, usually discontinuing the sessions impulsively without informing the therapist. When, with more maturity, Sylvie proposed a mutually agreed-upon date for termination of regular therapy sessions, the therapist left the door open for further courses of treatment, which it was anticipated Sylvie would need.

SUMMARY

Treating borderline personality disorder is a challenging and difficult experience for the psychotherapist. Yet, when a borderline patient recovers, it can provide one of the most gratifying moments in our professional lives. With other patients, we always wonder whether change was due to external events, our own ministrations, or time alone. With the borderline, one has a stronger sense that therapy has *happened*. A successful treatment is often a life and death struggle, with life emerging as the victor.

6

Narcissistic Personality Disorder

We are mostly narcissists, and only in a few, not always with felicitous results, is narcissism overcome (broken, crushed, annihilated, nothing less will serve) by religious discipline or psychoanalysis.

—Iris Murdoch

Narcissistic Personality Disorder (NPD) is characterized by a grandiose concept of the self and an exploitative relationship to others. The *DSM-IV* definition requires the presence of at least five of the following specific criteria: grandiosity, preoccupation with fantasies of success, feelings of being special, requirement for admiration, a sense of entitlement, interpersonal exploitation, lack of empathy, envy, and arrogance.

NPD is a special challenge for therapists interested in the modification of personality traits. Narcissism is the paradigmatic example of ego-syntonic psychopathology. Patients with narcissistic traits are absorbed with themselves and attribute responsibility for their unhappiness to the outside world. Therapists therefore need to address interpersonal insensitivity as well as the tendency to shift blame from self to others.

PSYCHODYNAMIC THEORIES OF NPD

Twenty years ago, two prominent psychoanalysts, Kohut (1970, 1977) and Kernberg (1976), began to write extensively about narcissistic personality disorder. There may have been two reasons for this surge of clinical interest. First, patients requesting therapy seemed to present less often with classical neurotic symptoms and more often with character problems. Although this may only reflect a difference in how clinicians formulate problems, some therapists (e.g., Kohut 1977) have speculated that narcissistic personality is actually more prevalent in the modern world. Second, patients with narcissistic traits are unusually resistant to change and therefore constitute a fair percentage of our therapeutic failures.

Kohut's Self Psychology

Kohut (1970, 1977) viewed narcissistic pathology as rooted in one of two developmental scenarios. One involves a failure of empathy, and is associated with consistent parental failure to "mirror" the feelings of a child. A second involves a failure in idealization, with the child suffering a traumatic loss of a positive image of a parent.

The first dynamic is based on the principle that children need approving and validating feedback from their parents. Kohut hypothesized that children develop a "cohesive self" by internalizing these mirroring responses over time. On the other hand, the absence of these responses leaves the child feeling alone and sorely lacking in inner cohesion. Grandiosity then develops as a defense against this sense of fragility. The adult narcissist might therefore be thought of like a child who thinks, "If no one can take care of me, then I will take care of myself." This mechanism helps to account for the narcissist's lack of interest in other people. The problem with narcissistic defenses is that they are innately fragile, requiring the constant reinforcement of attention from others. Thus, narcissists develop a pattern of neediness in their relationships that Kohut (1977) termed as *mirror-hungry,* involving a constant search for empathic and approving figures.

In Kohut's second scenario, the child is prematurely required to give up an idealization of a parent. Although we all go through this process, it is difficult to lose a sense of security too early in life. Unable to feel protected, the child feels alone and searches for a replacement who *can* be idealized. Kohut thought that narcissistic patients can show features of both these dynamic processes.

Kohut's approach to treatment followed logically from these ideas. The therapist's primary tasks are to empathize with patients and to accept their idealizations. Each time a patient feels misunderstood or disappointed, interpretations are used to show how these reactions reflect past experiences. Kohut's method leads to a rather long therapy, in the course of which the patient gradually internalizes the empathic responses of the therapist until the self attains sufficient cohesion, at which point narcissism should be expressed in healthier ways.

Self psychology introduced a number of useful and influential ideas to psychotherapy. However, there are four points that demand criticism: (1) The theory lacks support from empirical research in child development. (2) It takes no account of biologically determined individual differences in personality. (3) It emphasizes the failure to obtain emotional validation at the expense of the factor of parental indulgence. (4) The effectiveness of the therapeutic method has never been examined empirically.

Kernberg's Theory of Pathological Narcissism

Otto Kernberg (1976) sees narcissism as aggressive rather than defensive. He therefore makes fewer direct links between childhood experience and narcissistic personality in adulthood. The theory of *internalized object relations* emphasizes distortions within the psyche that create a view of the world that makes empathy, concern, or love impossible. The therapist's primary task is to point out to the patient this distorted perception of reality. Over time, confrontations and interpretations produce intrapsychic change.

Kernberg takes a refreshingly unsentimental attitude, perceiving the narcissist not just as a misunderstood person, but as potentially hostile and exploitative. Although his concept of constitutional differences in aggression is not rooted in trait theory, Kernberg takes biological differences in personality into account. One can, however, criticize Kernberg's formulations for using a complex metapsychological theoretical framework that has never been tested. Moreover, Kernberg's method of treatment leads to a lengthy therapy that has not yet been subjected to research about its effectiveness.

A MULTIDIMENSIONAL APPROACH TO NPD

This chapter will present an alternative theory of NPD, using a multidimensional framework that takes into account biological, psychological, and social factors in the etiology of the disorder.

Narcissistic personality is an exaggeration of underlying narcissistic traits. These traits, like other dimensions of normal personality, are influenced by genetic factors (Livesley et al. 1993); indeed, narcissism has a rather high rate of heritability (62 percent). In the absence of narcissistic traits, NPD will not develop. Thus, we do not see narcissistic pathology in individuals who are constitutionally self-effacing, cautious, or socially anxious.

We do not know the precise mechanisms by which narcissistic traits are amplified by experience. As pointed out by Millon and Davis (1996), therapists seem to believe in two contradictory ideas: that parents can make their children narcissistic either by spoiling them or by neglecting and criticizing them. However, there need not be any single pathway or specific abnormality of parenting leading to NPD.

Unlike borderline patients, narcissistic patients and their families have not been subject to research. Before embarking on such a program, we would first need a useful measure of narcissistic pathology. Gunderson (1994) has done some preliminary work in this direction, developing a semi-structured instrument—the Diagnostic Interview for Narcissism (DIN).

In many ways, narcissism can be thought of as exaggerated individualism, a trait that is highly rewarded in modern societies (Millon and Davis 1996, Paris 1996). The contemporary social context therefore helps to explain some of the current interest in narcissistic pathology. However, not all societies regard being self-centered as being a good thing. In particular, traditional societies (Lerner 1958) are structured to suppress narcissism, shaping children to put family and community ahead of their own personal goals. These priorities lead to a low rate of impulsive personality disorders in highly cohesive societies. For example, antisocial personality, which has features in common with NPD, is extremely rare in both Taiwan (Hwu et al. 1989) and Japan (Sato and Takeichi 1993). It makes sense to assume that children brought up to submit to the authority of the family and the community will be less likely to have narcissistic traits amplified. NPD is much more likely to develop in families that either allow or actively encourage their children to be self-centered.

HOW THERAPY CAN REINFORCE NARCISSISM

A problem that often goes unrecognized by therapists is that the very process of conducting psychotherapy has an innate tendency to reinforce narcissism. Narcissistic personality traits are usually ego-syntonic. Narcissists expect to be treated by everyone as special. They believe that most rules need not apply to them. They lack empathy and understand only dimly their effect on other people. It is therefore not very surprising that they are difficult patients for psychotherapists. However, there are other factors above and beyond the nature of narcissistic pathology that make therapy in NPD problematic. Treatment is made more difficult by factors intrinsic to the therapeutic enterprise. In other words, psychotherapy can be part of the problem.

Psychotherapy focuses the attention of patients on their

internal emotional states and needs and therefore encourages some degree of self-absorption. This is the main reason it has an intrinsic tendency to reinforce narcissism. Thinking more about oneself is a good development in patients who are insufficiently narcissistic. In fact, patients who have never given enough attention to their own needs may benefit, almost automatically, from the process of therapy. On the other hand, encouraging self-absorption, raising assertiveness, or increasing self-esteem in patients who already have a high level of these traits may not necessarily be helpful.

Narcissistic patients often enjoy coming to therapy. They are provided with the exclusive attention of an expert and may boast to their friends about the deep insights they are obtaining. They may even act, at least for a while, like a "good patient." Unfortunately, being in therapy is not sufficient by itself to produce behavioral change.

Narcissistic patients often believe that their personalities do not need to change very much, that it is other people who should change. Up to a point, this attitude is not necessarily maladaptive. In modern society, moderate levels of narcissistic traits increase adaptation. Well-functioning people need enough narcissism to assert their needs effectively. Thinking well of oneself without brooding unduly on one's defects tends to be associated with success and achievement. However, narcissistic patients come for treatment when these traits stop working for them. The presenting problems most often involve troubled interpersonal relationships.

Beyond a certain point, narcissistic traits prevent us from getting adequate input about our behavior from other people. We need other people to tell us about our strong and weak points. Grandiosity interferes with this process. The narcissistic patient manipulates others into providing positive feedback, while discouraging negative feedback through angry responses to any criticism. Without input from other people, we cannot develop mature interpersonal relationships. Without real concern for others, intimate attachments tend to be unstable. Finally, narcissistic patients often lack persistence, a personality trait without which success in life is often ephemeral.

VALIDATION, CONFRONTATION, AND GUILT

It follows from the above discussion that any effective therapeutic approach to NPD will require therapists to confront patients about their grandiosity. We need to delineate all the negative consequences of grandiose traits. The technical problem is how to make useful confrontations without hurting the patient and producing narcissistic rage.

Kohut (1970, 1977) thought that *empathizing* with patients is, in the long run, sufficient to reduce grandiosity. The theory of self psychology assumes that internalizing empathic responses increases inner cohesion. Therapy therefore becomes a kind of re-parenting, with the narcissist's feelings consistently validated by the therapist.

There is no doubt that therapists need to be tactful with patients. Often this means making a "sandwich," in which validating comments are the bread and confrontations the filling. However, it is probably not true that providing empathy, by itself, tames grandiosity. It is even doubtful whether those espousing self psychology actually practice in this way unless we are willing to expand the usual way we think about empathy. In his last book, Kohut (1984) humorously described a confrontation with a patient who had a habit of driving dangerously on the highway. Kohut announced that he would now give the most profound interpretation of the entire analysis: "You are a complete idiot!" This quasi-parental response might have been more empathic than any discussion of the patient's lack of mirroring from his parents.

The belief that grandiosity is rooted in low self-esteem makes us reluctant to confront our patients. Yet it remains an open question whether therapists treating NPD should aim to increase or decrease their patients' self-esteem. It is common in the therapeutic community to assume that when people feel better about themselves, they will behave better. As pointed out by Dawes (1994), there is scant evidence for this hypothesis. The problem with having a positive view of oneself is that this opinion may be quite unjustified. People with high self-esteem can be inconsiderate while those with low self-esteem can be paragons of virtue. Although we have no clear evidence one way or the other, it is likely that people need to feel bad about their misbehavior in order to change. Moreover, in the long run, behaving well to others supports realistic rather than unrealistic feelings of self-esteem.

In other words, however unfashionable it is to say so in the contemporary world, there is nothing wrong with healthy guilt. One must distinguish, of course, between appropriate guilt for actions that hurt others and guilt that is neurotic and irrational. Unfortunately, psychotherapy has sometimes taken a stance aiming to liberate people from any kind of guilt.

Psychotherapists must always take into account the moral dimension to human behavior. There *are* good and bad actions. Using any moral compass, we are ultimately judged not by our intentions but by our actions. In dealing with narcissistic pathology, therefore, one cannot entirely avoid being a moralist. When therapists tell people not to feel bad about their behavior, they run the danger of reinforcing narcissism.

It follows that therapists should be cautious about giving patients the message that they deserve the best for themselves. We should avoid implying that bad behavior is understandable rather than simply wrong. Finally, we should reconsider the traditional refusal of therapists to take responsibility for the welfare of the patient's family. Too often, the family of the patient with NPD is seen as part of the problem rather than as people who have the misfortune to live with a narcissist.

In summary, we must be careful about validating the worldview of the narcissist. Sometimes we simply lack sufficient information to determine how narcissistic patients are behaving. Like borderline patients, they often present the therapist with a distorted picture of their interpersonal worlds. It takes a good deal of skill to read between the lines and reconstruct what is actually going on. Sometimes the picture can only be clarified by interviewing key informants.

THE PSYCHOTHERAPIST'S VIEW
OF THE HUMAN CONDITION

There is another reason behind the reluctance of therapists to confront patients with their misbehavior. We are trained to see bad actions as motivated by negative experiences in the past. This view of the human condition makes everyone into a kind of victim. Thinking this way implies that each of us has a "true self" or an "inner child" that is all good. Only bad experiences make us bad.

Since the Second World War, this kind of romanticism has maintained a powerful influence on the thinking of psychotherapists. In its British incarnation, it is a major element of the object relations school of psychoanalysis. Thus, Winnicott (1958) thought that a child can develop a "false self," based on compliance with parental expectations, covering over the "true self," consisting of real and authentic emotions. Its American incarnation, Carl Rogers's client-centered therapy (Rogers 1961), was based on a belief in the essential goodness of people, such that therapists can be expected to respond to patients with "unconditional positive regard." The assumption was that most patients have a natural wish to become mature that only needs to be nurtured by their therapists.

This view was not shared by psychoanalysts such as Freud (1916) and Klein (1946), who were impressed by the extent to which children are capable of amorality and selfishness. An excessively sunny outlook on human nature will excuse almost any action. At best, the idea of an inner child is unprovable. At worst, it is sentimental nonsense.

There are useful lessons for therapists from the approach to narcissism taken by traditional religious organizations. In contemporary society, although religious feelings remain strong in many quarters, fewer and fewer people subscribe to the strict principles of organized religion. This is particularly the case among those requesting psychotherapy.

In many religious and philosophical traditions, what we now call narcissistic pathology was viewed as a serious barrier to moral behavior. The Greeks described hubris, while the Christians spoke of pride, but the underlying idea was much the same (Taylor 1992). Above and beyond specific theologies and dogmas, all religions encourage people to feel guilty when they act immorally. In summary, religion controls narcissistic behavior by encouraging individuals to believe in a deity before whom one must humble oneself. If one is to believe the stories one reads in the media of individuals who have dealt with scandal and disgrace through finding God, the positive effects of religion do not belong only to a historical past.

Psychotherapists can learn from the history of religion and from centuries of experience in traditional societies that encouraging healthy guilt *works*. However empathic therapists aim to be, they should not fear reinforcing guilt feelings for bad behavior.

When religious people behave better, they are rewarded by an increased sense of belonging to a community of believers that offers them an identity as well as a great deal of support and connection. The same sense of belonging is provided by any close-knit community and has historically defined the nature of traditional societies (Lerner 1958). When other people, whose good opinion one cherishes, are watching one's actions, one tends to restrain the tendency to be narcissistic.

Thus, traditional communities of all kinds tend to suppress narcissism. Traditional societies have a structure that does not promote what Lasch (1979) has called "the culture of narcissism." Although we are less likely to see the behaviors associated with NPD, there are other ways of expressing one's narcissism within a close-knit community. There will always be, of course, individuals with narcissistic traits in any community. Some will attain political or religious power and become responsible for criticizing other members of the community, while others can only tyrannize their families.

There are both positive and negative aspects to the tendency of traditional societies to encourage conformity. On the positive side are cohesion and the promise of belonging. On the negative side is frustration of those who are unusual, original, or individualistic, and who may not find a place in a traditional society and have to bear their frustration, or leave entirely.

But there are also both positive and negative aspects to the tendency of modern societies to promote individualism. On the positive side, many of us benefit from being able to develop ourselves as individuals. On the negative side, those who need more guidance and support are more likely to become alienated and lost.

In modern societies, the culture encourages individuals to put their own needs first. Traditional community structures, such as extended family and religious organizations, exert a decreasing influence on the young, particularly in urban areas (Millon 1993). More people are prepared to reject the comfort of living in a community in favor of life choices that promote their own personal goals. As a result, individuals with constitutionally high levels of narcissistic traits are more likely to give priority to their own interests.

In the modern world, particularly in large cities, there is greater anonymity and fewer consequences for one's actions. Moreover, urban life allows people to choose companions who validate their own points of view. Whereas our task is to show patients that their difficulties lie within themselves and not in the failure of other people to appreciate them properly, other people in their lives may be telling them to value themselves as highly as possible.

Even if narcissism is becoming more common, not everyone with grandiose traits comes to therapy. As long as the outside society continues to reward these traits, many people will escape the consequences of their narcissism. We only see those for whom the price has become too high.

We cannot, of course, offer our patients membership in a religious community. Moreover, with the notable exception of Alcoholics Anonymous and other twelve-step programs, which continue to use some traditional religious terminology, therapists cannot ask people to behave better by submitting themselves to a higher power. The only way we can convince narcissists to change is by demonstrating to them that their behavior makes *them* unhappy. In this context, the restraints on narcissism boil down to a purely pragmatic question: To what extent can one pursue personal goals without undergoing negative consequences?

Being considerate of others is a pragmatic choice. Acting in this way usually makes us more successful at work and more likely to develop a supportive social network. Thus, behaving better leads to being loved while behaving badly leads to being alone. Ultimately, this is our best leverage for modifying narcissistic traits.

FAMILY VALUES AND THERAPIST VALUES

Psychotherapists as a group are just as influenced as anyone else, if not more so, by the individualistic values of modern society. Moreover, the entire therapeutic enterprise is oriented toward goals such as encouraging assertiveness and validating perceived needs. This creates an implicit bias, giving priority to the needs of the individual over those of the family or the community. It may be no accident that psychotherapy as a method appeared at the very moment in history when traditional social structures were most rapidly breaking down (Lasch 1979). The individualistic bias of psychotherapy is particularly strong in North America, where it reflects the value system of the culture as a whole (Frank and Frank 1991, Varenne 1996).

In the last thirty years, the impact of modernity has steadily accelerated. As the influence of organized religion has declined, and as most people have experienced unprecedented levels of geographical and social mobility, individualism has become even stronger. Cultural narcissism encourages people to actualize themselves as opposed to living up to external ideals.

It is likely that this trend will continue, although it is balanced by a backlash from those who advocate a return to the traditional values associated with family and community. One might measure some of these social trends by noting the output of writers of best-selling columns and books in the area of popular psychology. Therapists may not read these books but they cannot escape being influenced by the social trends they represent. In modern society, psychotherapy has taken over some of the roles that used to belong to organized religion. Thus, inspirational books combining psychology and religion are popular, as demonstrated by an all-time best seller *The Road Less Traveled* (Peck 1985). Popular psychologists also offer the message that we should control our narcissism, and that doing as we please is morally and practically wrong (see Schlesinger 1996).

Clinicians have their own values and beliefs that are part of the subculture of psychotherapy. Most of us strongly support individual autonomy and view family and social networks in terms of how well they meet the needs of the individual. This value stands in contrast to that of traditional societies, which expect individuals to sacrifice their interests to the larger aims of the family and community.

All psychotherapists must therefore define where they stand on the question of family values. One issue of great clinical importance is how we feel about divorce. Of course, many divorces are both necessary and unavoidable and every psychotherapist has had the experience of helping patients separate from impossible marriages. However, divorce often affects innocent parties. We can no longer take the naive position that marital breakdown is usually good for the children. Research does show that when people are openly fighting, the children are usually better off immediately after a separation (Rutter and Rutter 1993). However, many divorces occur in circumstances where children were under the impression that their parents were happy, so they experience the breakup of the family as a traumatic surprise. In these cases, there can be a higher rate of negative long-term consequences, some of which may not be apparent until many years later (Hetherington et al. 1985, Wallerstein 1989).

The extremely high divorce rate in our society is a direct consequence of individualistic values. If one believes that unhappily married people have a right to a better relationship, divorce is logical. Therapists who share these values are therefore more likely to encourage their patients to find new partners. Therapists' approaches to family integrity will depend in part on their own life experiences, such as whether they themselves have been divorced.

There are also intrinsic biases in individual psychotherapy that make divorce a likely outcome. When patients tell us they are treated badly by a spouse, our knee-jerk reaction can be to validate these feelings. It requires a special effort to find out what patients are doing to provoke the other person. Therapists who take the trouble to interview couples and families will often be surprised as to how different reality can be from perceptions.

Moreover, if treatment from a spouse is similar to treatment from a significant person in the past, we may say, explicitly or implicitly, "Why are you repeating this pattern?" Although this is often a legitimate question, it tends to imply that the choice of partner was probably wrong and that the patient should consider whether to jettison the relationship.

Whenever we emphasize what individuals "deserve," we support feelings of entitlement. When we tell patients that their problems reflect a deficit in self-esteem, and that an unhappy childhood has made them feel undeserving of a better life, the implicit message is: consider yourself more and consider the needs of others less.

These messages might be helpful for individuals with an insufficient level of narcissism. Patients with anxious cluster personality disorders are excessively self-effacing and rarely in danger of dominating other people. However, narcissistic patients, with their serious deficiencies in empathy, are likely to be difficult spouses and inadequate parents. They often change partners and then act in the same way with a new cast of characters. It is no accident that, statistically speaking, divorce rates go up with each succeeding marriage (Riley 1991). There must be a number of individuals with NPD among the multiply divorced.

Many narcissistic patients are unwilling to marry and may leave behind them a string of unhappy lovers. This failure to commit can be protective—both for themselves and for others. Moreover, marriages between two narcissistic individuals are often doomed from the start (Lansky 1991).

In treating patients who have experienced divorce, therapy should try to increase the likelihood that any subsequent relationships will be more successful. If there are children involved, we should also try to help our narcissistic patients be better parents. Even for those who have given their families insufficient priority in the past, there is always the possibility of redress.

WORKING WITH NARCISSISM: STRATEGY

Let us now apply the general principles of our approach to personality disorders described in Chapter 4 to patients with NPD. Therapy works with narcissistic traits to reverse their amplification. Reducing levels of grandiosity should lead to better social adaptation.

Triage is necessary to identify those patients who justify the investment of our clinical energy and time. It is better to sift out in advance those who cannot work in therapy than to spend years on fruitless and frustrating efforts. The treatable patients with NPD are those who suffer enough to realize the need for real change, and can, at least to some extent, join with the therapist in observing their own behavior critically.

Clinicians reading this chapter can no doubt bring to mind narcissistic patients they have known who could not accept even the gentlest confrontation and responded to the therapist's desire to help with contempt. Patients who never form a strong working alliance are probably not suitable for psychotherapy; ideally, they should be triaged out at the time of evaluation. In practice, we may sometimes be unable to recognize intractable patients until they have undergone a trial of therapy.

That personality-disordered patients can be untreatable is not always stated openly in texts on psychotherapy. Too many writers prefer to attribute difficulties in treating patients to deficiencies in the therapist. Thus, problems can be ascribed either to the therapist's countertransference or to a failure to understand patients deeply enough. The implication is that if you are as well trained, as thoroughly analyzed, and as knowledgeable as some therapeutic guru, you should be able to treat almost anybody with success. As we have seen in Chapter 3, the empirical evidence points just the other way: it is the characteristics of patients, not therapists, that are the most important predictors of the outcome of therapy.

Since patients with NPD think of themselves as special, they may not be satisfied with the usual, banal reasons for seeking treatment. They may prefer to present themselves as unusually interesting cases for therapy as opposed to being ordinary sufferers. Initially, the evaluating clinician may be puzzled by the vagueness of their symptomatology. Narcissistic patients may present with such chief complaints as, "I want to learn more about myself," or, "I need to finish my analysis." Such comments should make therapists instantly vigilant. In most cases, the real reasons for seeking help will emerge. They typically involve an inability to establish meaningful relationships, the breakup of a relationship, or a major disappointment in work.

Ultimately, narcissism leads to tragedy in life—for patients, and for their significant others. Life experiences inevitably batter down everyone's grandiosity. We must all deal with disappointment and failure and come to terms with our own limitations as well as those of other people. If we do not do so, our lives will be very unhappy indeed. As shown by Torgersen

(1995), patients with NPD have a surprisingly high level of dysphoria, largely because their close relationships are unsatisfactory. In spite of their overtly high opinions of themselves, narcissistic patients often seek treatment after a failure of intimacy.

In the work area, narcissists can be promising or even brilliant. As Miller (1981) suggests, one cannot become narcissistic unless one has some special talent or quality that the outside world recognizes. Some narcissists are very successful indeed and have serious difficulties only in their intimate relationships. Others fail to meet the expectations they create and are underachievers. Such individuals usually believe that it is sufficient to have potential in life. Hard work is not really necessary for some narcissists, who may not be willing to change direction to meet the needs of other people and may alienate co-workers by failing to respond to social cues.

Many narcissists are unpleasantly surprised when their superiors indicate that their performance is not up to par. Unfortunately, responding to negative feedback with anger only makes solving problems more difficult. Narcissistic patients need to understand that other people's evaluations of them are usually valid.

Narcissistic pathology has its most dramatic effects on intimate attachments. Torgersen (1995) found that patients with NPD have a low rate of marriage and a very high rate of divorce as well as an overall instability in long-term relationships. This is probably explained by the failure of narcissists to take other people's feelings into account, an inability to empathize with others that often leads to disaster. A primary goal of therapy, therefore, is to help patients to understand and to consider the needs of others. This often involves interventions along the following lines: "It was understandable that you got upset, but what do you think the other person was feeling in that situation?"

Narcissistic traits decline over long courses of therapy. We do not always know whether this is due to developmental increases in maturity, the cumulative impact of life experiences, or treatment. Thus, the "burnout" of Cluster B disorders such as antisocial personality (Black et al. 1995) and borderline personality (Paris 1994), as well as the maturation of ego defenses over time (Vaillant 1977), are all consistent with reductions of narcissism over time. In most people, youthful grandiosity is reduced by life's inevitable disappointments. Kernberg (1976) has even suggested that many narcissistic patients only become treatable in middle age.

Although the duration of therapy for NPD is usually not short, therapy need not be entirely open-ended. It is not cost-effective to see patients interminably. As discussed in the previous chapter on BPD, we might therefore consider providing narcissistic patients intermittent courses of psychotherapy.

WORKING WITH NARCISSISM: TACTICS

As discussed in Chapter 4, working with traits does not require modification of standard therapeutic methods. Once we invite people into treatment, therapy takes on a certain rhythm. Patients talk about whatever is foremost on their minds, how they have been feeling, and what has happened in their lives since the last session. The role of the therapist is to comment on the patient's thoughts, feeling, and behaviors.

There are two important differences between the model being advocated here and the recommendations of previous writers on NPD. The first concerns the use of historical information. There is a particular danger in applying an approach based on the primacy of childhood experience to the narcissist. Patients with NPD tend to view the past as a drama in which they are sympathetic protagonists who have been misunderstood and mistreated by parents who were at best well-meaning, and at worst malevolent. This view of history is self-serving, and can be used as an "abuse excuse" to justify inconsiderate or exploitative behavior.

In patients with NPD, it is therefore particularly important for therapy sessions to focus on present conflicts with other people. Although it can be useful to point out parallels between recent incidents and past events in the patient's life, the most crucial interventions involve demonstrating the maladaptive consequences of the patient's behavior. Only then can the patient consider developing constructive and adaptive alternatives.

Second, the model proposed here does not make the transference a major focus of therapy. The approach therefore differs from that advocated by Kohut (1977), who used patients' reactions to the therapist's failures of empathy to demonstrate their fragile self-esteem and to reconstruct how empathic failures in patients' pasts made them vulnerable to feeling misunderstood. The model also diverges from that of Kernberg (1976), who spotlighted patients' hostile and exploitative attitudes to the therapist as a way of demonstrating their problems with other people. This is not to say that these interventions are not valuable—they most certainly can be. The issue is one of priorities.

Transference phenomena can be best used as examples of problems paralleling those in the patient's outside life. The problem with focusing on transference is that positive experiences in therapy are not always generalized. What happens within the haven of treatment need not be mirrored with other, less protective figures in one's life. Changing the patient's behavior inside therapy does not assure that similar changes will occur elsewhere. It is quite possible to have a good relationship with a therapist and a bad one with almost everyone else.

Since the work of psychotherapy in NPD concerns problems with other people, the first step involves the identification of maladaptive patterns. Tactful confrontations are needed for patients to perceive and acknowledge these problems prior to solving them. As discussed in Chapter 4, these will usually consist of questions, such as, "Have you thought of any other way to understand what happened?" or, just a bit more force-fully, "I wonder if there might be another way to look at this story."

The therapist must actively help the narcissistic patient to see interpersonal conflicts from other people's point of view. Individuals with NPD may have to be taught this skill. Otherwise, they tend to attribute other people's reactions to neglect or malevolence. Narcissistic patients are often poor at the inter-personal tasks most people take for granted—knowing what other people want and negotiating compromises so that each person gets to meet some portion of their needs. At the same time, patients need to see that self-serving behaviors work to their own disservice. The most mileage comes from this type of confrontation.

Narcissism interferes with normal learning processes about human relationships. When every reverse in life is interpreted as someone else's failing, we cannot change. Patients with low empathy fail to observe how their behavior affects other people and present distorted or self-serving versions of events to the therapist. Unless narcissistic patients can take responsibility for their mistakes, they continue to make the same ones.

Therapy in NPD takes time because these adaptive skills are not readily learned and because maladaptive responses must also be unlearned. The patience of a good therapist will be tested as the patient gets it wrong over and over again. With hard work and persistence, enough progress can be made for the patient to begin to experience some of the rewards of nonexploitative human relationships.

CASE EXAMPLE 1: ROBERT

History

Robert was a junior executive who presented for treatment with complaints of loneliness and difficulty getting along with other people. At 28, he was progressing in his career but had never had a long-term intimate relationship with a woman.

Much of Robert's energy was refocused from the real world to the world of his imagination. His fantasies largely concerned fame, fortune, and sexual conquest. He imagined himself living in a penthouse, surrounded by a series of women so beautiful and desirable that other men would envy him.

In real life, Robert objectified women in such a blatant fashion that he was often rejected. Few women wanted to see him more than once. He wanted them to focus on *his* needs so that he would not have to think about ways of courting or pleasing. Robert was addicted to pornographic videos. He spent a great deal of his money paying strippers who performed in bars and once actually attempted to have a relationship with one of these women.

In his work, Robert was ambitious but uninspired. His problems in that sphere usually involved conflicts with supervisors who failed to recognize him as having unique abilities.

Robert had grown up as the eldest of three sons in a middle-class family. As a child, he had an aggressive, irritable, and impulsive temperament. He was very demanding with his parents and intensely jealous of his brothers, to whom he was often physically aggressive. His father, a small businessman, was very concerned with his image in the community and taught the children to present a good face to strangers. His mother, who was in agreement with these principles, often criticized Robert harshly and hurtfully for his misbehavior.

If no other negative events had occurred, Robert would probably have developed into an adult with only a few problematical traits. However, Robert's parents, most particularly his father, also presented models of narcissistic behavior. When Robert was 12, his father's personality changed dramatically. He took a mistress and brought home marijuana, offering to smoke it with his sons. He spent money unwisely, taking a large sum that had been left in trust for Robert out of the bank. The father then lost his business, after which he left his wife and went to live with his mistress. The rest of Robert's adolescence was spent with his mother, who was impoverished, embittered, and too preoccupied with her own troubles to attend to her children's needs.

As a result, Robert felt that he could trust no one. He concluded that success was the best revenge. What he needed most was to become rich. He obtained an M.B.A., focusing his energy on getting ahead. He succeeded in making a good living but still felt emotionally empty.

Robert's sense of entitlement led him to be involved in a number of minor crimes. A woman with whom he had a brief love affair dropped him because he was insufficiently attentive to her needs. He went to her apartment and stole several items of her jewelry, which he never used but kept in his house. On another occasion, when his own apartment was broken into, he made fraudulent insurance claims that netted him thousands of dollars. He felt very little guilt about these episodes, rationalizing that he needed to provide himself with compensation even when the outside world could not.

Therapy

Suitability for Treatment

A number of factors in Robert's case pointed to his treatability. His overall level of functioning outside intimate relationships was good. His defenses were not rigid. Although he was furious at a world that he felt had cheated him, he recognized that his own behavior was making the situation worse.

Alliance and Structure

In spite of Robert's grandiosity, he had few problems forming an alliance in therapy. He formed a stable transference to the therapist, idealizing him, and making him into the good father he had lost.

Modifying Narcissistic Traits

Confrontations of Maladaptive Behaviors

Much of the work of therapy involved confrontations. The therapist consistently pointed out the maladaptiveness and negative consequences of Robert's behavior. Thus, although he fantasized about a perfect relationship with a woman, he was, in the end, not able to establish any attachments at all. No woman would put up with an absence of any concern for her welfare. A stripper might be willing to play up to his fantasies, and only then for the brief time during which she was being paid for her services.

The Psychodynamic Prong: Examining the Historical Context

These confrontations had more impact when placed in a historical context. The therapist pointed out that the patient had been radically disappointed by both his parents, who had not met his needs for support and understanding. He may have actually required extra help from his parents to deal with his impulsive and emotional temperament. In his early life, Robert had been overindulged. Later, when no one stepped in to tame his grandiosity, his narcissism was amplified by neglect.

The therapist pointed out how Robert responded to the world as if he were still dealing with his family. His inability to depend on anyone and his need to hit back whenever he was disappointed might have been the only ways to survive his traumatic adolescence but they were inappropriate behaviors for a grown man.

The Behavioral Prong: Development of Adaptive Alternatives

The first achievement of the therapy was the stabilization of Robert's work situation. Achieving on the job provided him with a haven from more difficult problems in interpersonal relationships. Once, he got himself in serious trouble by rudely contradicting one of his supervisors at a committee meeting. Robert realized that, whatever the merits of his case, his behavior was out of line, and he made an apology that effectively patched the matter up. He needed many more confrontations from the therapist about similar incidents. For example, he had to stop himself from manipulating business records in a way that would provide more rewards for himself and less for everybody else in his office.

The most dramatic events of the therapy centered around a love affair that began about a year after treatment started. Robert met Cora, a young woman who managed a hotel for her father, an enormously rich builder. Robert imagined himself leaving his own firm, and working for a wealthy father-in-law.

In the initial stages of their relationship, Robert and Cora related to each other much like children. Yet in spite of their symbiotic attachment, they were unskilled in listening to and understanding each other. Whenever Cora was preoccupied, either with her work, family, or friends, Robert would become enraged. Their quarrels escalated, sometimes to the point of becoming physical brawls. Cora retaliated by starting a lesbian affair with a close friend. Robert had actually suggested at one point that they have a threesome, but when Cora acted first, he felt crushed and excluded. He tried to blacken Cora's name by spreading the story all over town, and they parted on the worst of terms.

At first, all Robert could do in therapy was to express his fury about Cora's mistreatment. Over time, he began to understand how he had gone wrong. He was even able to accept his own share of the responsibility for Cora's infidelity. Robert eventually acknowledged that Cora's lover had displaced him because she was a maternal woman who was a better listener than Robert had ever been.

Making Better Use of Existing Traits

Robert was an ambitious man. Yet, he was a consistent under-achiever because grandiosity interfered with actual performance. As he improved, he began to pay serious attention to the expectations of his job and discovered that when he scaled down his goals, he could actually gain pleasure from persisting at a task and completing it.

Outcome

At the end of the therapy, which lasted for two years, Robert was clearly functioning better. He had been promoted at work. Although he was not yet in another serious relationship, he no longer insisted on dating women who were beautiful and rich. When he met people, he was interested in what they were like and how different they might be from him. Robert eventually discovered that it was interesting to know what other people feel.

CASE EXAMPLE 2: GORDON

History

Gordon was a 35-year-old graduate student in art history. His chief complaint concerned an inability to maintain intimacy with women. Most recently, a five-year, live-in relationship with a fellow graduate student had ended in disaster.

Gordon had never been faithful to Rachel for very long. Most of the transgressions were casual affairs. Gordon was a good-looking man who, in spite of his advancing years, retained the angelic look of a hippie and was usually able to pick up women without difficulty. Moreover, as a teaching assistant, Gordon had many opportunities to meet undergraduates who found his intellectual and bohemian manner fascinating.

Over the last six months, Rachel, who had been oblivious to Gordon's behavior, was totally preoccupied with writing her thesis. She became emotionally unavailable and rarely left the house. Rachel had helped Gordon through many crises of his own and had transferred to the same university in order to be able to live with him. She therefore expected Gordon to support her through her own time of difficulty.

Gordon's view of the matter was different. He felt trapped in the apartment with Rachel and could only think of how to make his escape. After a few casual affairs, he began a more serious involvement with Dawn, a 21-year-old student in one of his classes. Gordon was never able to describe his new lover to the therapist in terms of her personal qualities. Rather, Dawn was portrayed only as a pre-Raphaelite image, a young woman of extraordinary beauty with a pure and innocent soul. When a fellow student with a grudge against Gordon reported the facts of this affair to Rachel, there was an explosion and Gordon was forced to move out.

Gordon had been brought up in a rather small and isolated community. His father, a teacher and a war veteran, was an unsuccessful man who had tried to live on his past glories. This strategy earned little admiration from Gordon's mother, who was carrying out a flagrant love affair with the town mayor. Gordon sympathized with his father but could not respect him for accepting such humiliation. He deeply resented his mother, who on several occasions had used activities with her son as a cover for her liaison.

Gordon left home at age 18 and spent the next two years traveling around North America. Since he was young, strikingly good-looking, and clever, he had many picaresque adventures on which he could dine out for many years afterwards. Over the coming years, Gordon lived with many different women and sired at least three illegitimate children. He maintained intermittent contact with only one of them, a ten-year-old daughter in a distant city.

In his late 20s, Gordon went back to university as a mature student. This is where he met Rachel, the first person in his life in whose presence he felt awe. This was because Rachel was a capable and organized woman; she played an important role in inspiring Gordon to pursue his graduate studies.

However, at 35, Gordon's attempt to remain eternally youthful was failing. He was under pressure to complete his thesis on the pre-Raphaelite painters but had barely begun. Rachel, the great stabilizing influence of his life, had left him. He saw very little of his family. He had very few close male friends. The downhill course of his life became sufficiently apparent that he sought treatment.

Therapy

Suitability for Treatment

Gordon, though a late bloomer, had a history of sufficient success in his work to be admitted to graduate school. Although his intimate relationships had proved ultimately unsuccessful, he had been able to remain attached for long periods to several women.

Alliance and Structure

Gordon's therapy was divided into two separate periods. In the first, the main focus was the loss of his relationship with Rachel. To build an alliance, the therapist took pains to empathize with Gordon's pain. In the second phase, the therapy focused on why he had been unable to act in a way to maintain this important relationship.

Modifying Narcissistic Traits

Confrontations of Maladaptive Behaviors

The therapist made confrontation of Gordon's entitlement the primary issue in treatment. Gordon needed to be the central focus of a woman's desire but made little effort to understand her point of view. The therapist asked Gordon to consider more carefully the effect of his behavior on the women in his life. Although Gordon had little capacity for guilt, he could recognize that his way of handling intimacy led to disaster. Moreover, as Gordon aged, he could expect to have less choice of partners. Ultimately, unless he could change, he would end up empty and alone.

The Psychodynamic Prong: Examining the Historical Context

From a historical point of view, it was clear that Gordon, ever since his difficult childhood experiences with his mother, had been suspicious and hostile of any woman who might be in a position to control him. Although he could hardly have chosen a partner more different from his mother than Rachel was, Gordon had responded to her in much the same way, by taking revenge on his betrayer.

The Behavioral Prong: Development of Adaptive Alternatives

Gordon was not likely to settle down with any woman for many years to come. Treatment might, nonetheless, reduce the intensity of his narcissism. The primary goal was therefore to help him to mourn for Rachel and then to encourage him to find a more stable source of self-esteem. This involved setting aside his interest in visiting clubs with the aim of initiating new love affairs, and beginning to work seriously on his thesis. After a year of therapy, both of these goals were achieved, and Gordon left the country with the intention of continuing his research in England.

The second act of the treatment began when Gordon returned from his year abroad. He had had a productive time in London. At the same time, he had kept up a regular correspondence with Dawn. However, understandably, she had not waited for him and became involved with someone her own age. When Dawn refused to have anything further to do with him, Gordon experienced fury and humiliation. He reacted by superficially cutting his wrists, returning to the therapist's office as an emergency. Although Gordon now had to mourn another loss, this one involved a fantasy relationship as opposed to the real intimacy he had experienced in his years with Rachel.

The therapy continued to focus on Gordon's entitlement. Although he could not empathize with Dawn, he was asked to consider whether a woman of her age could have actually met his needs. The therapist also pointed out how Gordon's behavior toward women distracted him from his goal of establishing his academic career. Before attaining intimacy, he would first have to establish himself as a person in his own right, that is, finish his Ph.D. and obtain a job.

The therapist emphasized that Gordon's need for adulation from a woman was an addiction he had to overcome. This would have to involve going cold turkey and then finding substitute satisfactions. Gordon was more receptive to these messages than he had been in the first stage of treatment, and began to work on his thesis. He was now living alone, going out with friends, and having only a few casual affairs.

Making Better Use of Existing Traits

Gordon's grandiosity was fed by domination and seduction of women. Therapy helped him refocus his goals on satisfactions that were more manageable, even if he might consider them banal. Gordon needed a stable source of self-esteem that would make it less necessary for him to prop himself up with romantic conquests. The unanswered long-term question was whether he would ever be able to settle for an exclusive relationship with a woman, in which case he would have to accept her limitations as well as his own.

Outcome

One year after the completion of his treatment, Gordon had completed his Ph.D. and begun academic work in another city.

He had no close ties to any woman and was ready to launch his career.

SUMMARY

The reader will no doubt note that, as shown in both of the above case examples, patients with narcissistic personality disorder do not always succeed in establishing stable intimate relationships. Some readers might think that the therapies described here should be thought of as the first phase of a "deeper" treatment intended to guide patients into true maturity. The burden of proof for this idea would lie with those who claim that doing so is actually possible.

This is not to say that narcissistic patients never achieve intimacy as a result of therapy. Some do, and many writers about psychotherapy present such case histories as typical examples of what treatment can accomplish. However, we need to resist the temptation to describe cases that, like a Victorian novel, always end with a happy marriage. These fairy tales can give other therapists the mistaken impression that the writer's results are much better than their own.

As we all know, not all long-term relationships are happy. Therefore, it is not clear why marriage need be viewed as a necessary or salutary outcome of therapy, particularly for those who have little talent for intimacy. Many patients with personality disorders need not be strongly encouraged to embark on marriage. For the narcissist, intimacy carries a particular risk. As suggested by Kernberg (1974), some patients only achieve a real capacity for love late in life, when the external environment no longer reinforces their narcissism. If the treatment is long enough, the therapist might be tempted to take credit for results that are more likely attributable to gradual social learning over time.

The cases described above represent the treatable end of the spectrum of narcissistic personality disorder. Not all patients are this manageable, and the most difficult cases test our mettle as clinicians. Nonetheless, limited outcomes can provide a reasonable degree of satisfaction for psychotherapists. Treatment can be considered successful when it helps narcissistic patients reduce their grandiosity and become more open to life's possibilities.

7

Histrionic Personality Disorder

By the end of the evening I had extricated myself from her
spell. She killed my admiration by her talk. Her role alone
preoccupies her. She invents dramas in which she always
stars.

—Anaïs Nin on June Miller

CLINICAL FEATURES

Histrionic personality disorder (HPD) is characterized by dramatic communication, an impressionistic cognitive style, and the sexualization of relationships. The *DSM-IV* definition requires the presence of at least five of the following criteria: a need to be the center of attention, inappropriate sexualization, shallow emotions, use of physical appearance to draw attention, impressionistic speech, theatricality, suggestibility, and a tendency to exaggerate the quality of intimacy in relationships.

This clinical picture is familiar to most psychotherapists. Patients with HPD usually seek treatment when they experience the failure of an important relationship. In an epidemiological study, Nestadt and colleagues (1990) found HPD to be frequently associated with a history of separation or divorce. We will discuss later in this chapter some of the reasons why intimate relationships in histrionic patients are particularly fragile.

HPD is a common diagnosis in clinical practice and has been shown in community studies to be highly prevalent, affecting about 2 percent of the population (Nestadt et al. 1990). Histrionic patients have a higher level of overall functioning than those with BPD (Nakao et al. 1992). However, all the disorders in Cluster B tend to overlap, and some clinical observers (e.g., Zetzel 1970) have speculated that histrionic and borderline pathology lie on a continuum. In clinical populations, the diagnosis is most frequently made among women (Chodoff 1982). The clinical description of histrionic personality is, in many respects, a caricature of femininity (Halleck 1967, Lerner 1974).

Epidemiological research (Nestadt et al. 1990) suggests that HPD could be equally common in males. The discrepancy could be explained if histrionic men are less likely to seek treatment than are women, or if they present with a clinical picture that is more likely to be labeled narcissistic. It is possible that all the disorders in Cluster B are biased by gender. At the severe end, the antisocial and borderline categories may represent male and female versions of the same disorder (Paris 1997b). At the less severe end, the narcissistic and histrionic categories reflect similar pathology.

THE TRAITS UNDERLYING HISTRIONIC BEHAVIOR

Costa and Widiger (1994), have applied the Five Factor Model of personality (see Chapter 1) to define the traits underlying HPD. Histrionics would be expected to be high in extraversion, high in neuroticism, and high in openness to experience.

The most striking feature in histrionic patients is their high level of extraversion. Extraverted people are gregarious and engaging and require a high level of stimulation. In extreme instances of this trait, people define themselves entirely through the reactions of other people. The extreme extravert also needs to be the center of attention in a social setting. In the population of young women in whom the diagnosis of HPD is usually made, the most obvious way to attract attention from the opposite sex is by flirting, so attachments become sexualized.

Neuroticism is another important characteristic of the histrionic patient. This trait makes individuals thin-skinned and emotionally labile, making them easily upset by their environment.

Openness to experience implies that a person is easily influenced by others in the environment, so this trait is associated with suggestibility. People with histrionic traits also tend to see the broad outlines of a situation rather than its details. Shapiro (1965) was the first to note this characteristically impressionistic cognitive style, which is now a diagnostic criterion for HPD in the *DSM*.

These traits also help account for some of the problems particular to the treatment of these patients. As a group, histrionics are engaging and emotionally open. This is why most therapists tend to see them, at least initially, as "good patients." Over time, the same traits can make them seem less desirable.

Histrionic patients rarely have trouble starting a session, and they usually tell a good story. Yet it is often difficult to get them to go beyond describing events and to introspect about their own emotions. Patients with HPD enjoy the therapy situation, in which they are clearly the center of attention. However, because they can be emotionally demanding, they can also leave treatment impulsively when frustrated. They initially idealize and flatter the therapist, responding to every comment as though it is a brilliant insight. Yet they can also become angry and resentful about the therapist's neutrality. Similar reactions will often have created difficulties in the patient's intimate relationships.

Ultimately, histrionic traits do not provide a good basis for lasting attachments. Patients with HPD rarely have trouble attracting lovers. Yet over time, the more they demand, the more other people pull away, a pattern that undermines the stability of relationships. The high rate of failed marriages and love affairs in HPD helps explain why these patients are unusually susceptible to depression (Slavney and McHugh 1974).

PATHWAYS FROM HISTRIONIC TRAITS TO DISORDERS

There has been hardly any systematic research on the psychological risk factors for HPD. In one of the few empirical studies examining this issue (Baker et al. 1992), individuals with strong histrionic traits reported that their parents were over-controlling while their family structures were low in cohesion. These findings are too general to be useful to clinicians. Thus, without more research, the discussion in this section will have to be rather speculative, basing conclusions largely on the author's clinical experience. It would, nonetheless, be interesting to test these hypotheses by conducting systematic studies of patients with histrionic personality.

What psychological factors in development could influence whether normal traits, such as extraversion, neuroticism, and openness to experience, become amplified to the level of a personality disorder? We can present several patterns here, some of which have been described in the clinical literature and others observed by the author in his therapy practice.

Triangular Family Dynamics

One of the best known psychodynamic patterns associated with histrionic traits in the literature is a family in which a woman feels an excessive closeness during childhood to her father, combined with an excessive distance from her mother (Zetzel 1970). Some observers might term these issues oedipal. However, there is another way of looking at the phenomena.

Research shows that parental neglect as well as parental overprotection are risk factors for a variety of psychological problems (Parker 1983). These findings are not specific to any one disorder. Their general implication is that psychological health is associated with successful individuation and that to achieve autonomy, children need to feel securely attached to both parents and to feel they can leave their parents without hurting them.

Family systems theory (Minuchin 1974) has introduced a useful construct, *triangulation*, which helps explain why children trapped within their family structures have difficulty individuating. Systems theory hypothesizes that children are most likely to obtain both emotional support and support for separation when their parents are happy with each other. When this is the case, neither of the parents needs emotional support from the children and both parents can be comfortable with a child's separation. The converse of this happy scenario involves marital discord between parents, which is the ultimate cause of problems in triangulation. When the parents are not getting along with each other, intergenerational alliances can form. Marital conflicts then become displaced into disagreements about the children, and parents form alliances with their children against each other.

These family patterns can have a long-term impact. Some authors (e.g., Hollender 1971, Zetzel 1971) have suggested that girls are more likely to turn to their fathers for love when they have difficulty bonding with their mothers. In most cases, though, a father, however idealized, is not fully available to the young girl as a secure base for attachment. The father whose daughter is the apple of his eye may treat her as a reflection of his own narcissism, selectively reinforcing her charm and seductiveness. However, such a response is ultimately unsatisfying and the daughter must seek compensation elsewhere. If she is extraverted and gregarious, she can readily find admiration from other men.

Absence of the Father

A second pattern that can be seen in histrionic patients is the physical absence of the father. Of course, in today's society with its epidemic of divorce, a large number of our patients suffer from this deficiency. However, an absent father may have one kind of effect on girls with histrionic traits and an entirely different effect on girls with an anxious temperament.

Many of the problems histrionic patients present in therapy concern the men in their lives. A father may often have been physically or emotionally absent but idealized and yearned for. In such cases, a young woman can grow up feeling deprived of paternal attention and mirroring. She may react to this situation by demanding special attention from every other man in her life. The search for a substitute father can become consuming. However, this is a role that no boyfriend or husband can adequately fulfill.

An instructive example of this pattern can be observed in the biography of the writer Anaïs Nin (Bair 1995). Nin had an unusually outgoing and creative personality. Her father, a classical musician, abandoned the family when Anaïs was ten years old. She began to write him a long letter in the hope of getting him to return. This missive eventually converted itself into a lifelong diary, several volumes of which have been published. As one can see from both the diaries and the biography, Nin's interests centered, to an unusual degree, around sexual conquest. Thus, she successfully seduced a series of psychoanalysts who attempted to treat her. Her life took a particularly bizarre twist when, at the age of 30, she re-contacted her father and began a sexual affair with him. Nin went over the top in ways that most histrionic women would never dream of.

Modeling of Histrionic Traits

A third pattern that can be seen in histrionic patients is a close and enmeshed relationship with a mother who is herself histrionic. In these cases, modeling from the mother encourages a daughter to seek male attention in the same way. This process will be further reinforced if the daughter also has an extraverted temperament.

*   *   *

These three patterns are not mutually exclusive, and there is no single psychological pathway to the amplification of histrionic traits. Moreover, the psychodynamics associated with HPD do not explain the disorder, since many women grow up with either overly close or overly distant relationships with their fathers and only a minority of them have histrionic traits, not to speak of a histrionic personality disorder.

Interactions between a pre-existing trait profile (extraversion, neuroticism, openness to experience) and one of these patterns of family dynamics may lead to HPD. Let us imagine how this process might work. The scenario would begin with a young girl who is charming, outgoing, and engaging. Let us also assume she is emotionally labile and imaginative. If she obtains secure love from her parents, she will become a striking and interesting woman and her adult relationships will remain reasonably stable. However, if she does not receive sufficient admiration from her parents, her need for attention will become amplified. As a child, she may learn that being cute obtains powerful rewards for her. At puberty, she discovers that overt sexuality earns her the attention she cannot find in her family. By adulthood, this pattern can be well ingrained. If the behavior associated with these traits becomes dysfunctional, that is, if it leads to superficial, unstable, and unhappy relationships, the young woman may come to meet the diagnostic criteria for HPD.

WORKING WITH HISTRIONIC TRAITS

Histrionic patients require a two-pronged strategy. From a historical perspective, HPD patients often offer us rich psychodynamic material. However, working with traits usually requires hard slogging.

Treatment must modify the traits underlying the disorder. The most important of these probably consists of excessive levels of extraversion. It is not adaptive to be in a position in which one's self-esteem consistently depends on attention bestowed by other people. For one thing, all of us suffer our inevitable share of rejections. Success in life requires us to develop what Winnicott (1965) termed "the capacity to be alone." Therapists need to help histrionic patients find ways to increase that capacity.

When neuroticism is also amplified, a high level of emotionality puts the patient even more at the mercy of the environment. For the emotionally labile person, every breeze is a storm. We tend to think of psychotherapy working best in patients who are emotionally expressive. However, since histrionic patients suffer from being overly emotional, therapists need to teach them to reflect on their feelings.

Openness to experience refers to an ability to be permeable to life experiences as well as the capacity to lose oneself in experience. Normally this trait can be entirely adaptive and is associated with characteristics ranging from strong emotional reactions to works of literature, art, and music to a love of foreign travel. However, this dimension, when sufficiently amplified, can develop into a failure to maintain proper boundaries between self and environment. In other words, histrionic patients have to know how to turn off stimulation from the outside world and look within themselves.

The cognitive-behavioral prong of therapy in HPD involves a kind of psychoeducational approach to teach patients how to become more autonomous. Finding alternate sources of support for self-esteem protects patients from excessive extraversion and buffers neuroticism and opennness. The examples below will show how therapy helps patients depend less on feedback from others and make more use of inner resources.

CASE EXAMPLE 1: GLORIA

History

Gloria presented for treatment at age 37 after the sudden and traumatic breakup of her marriage. After fifteen years, her husband had left her for another woman. Moreover, he had cut off all contact with her, refusing to have any dialogue except through lawyers. Gloria felt bewildered, humiliated, and devastated. She had a great deal of trouble sleeping and was seriously considering suicide.

Gloria was a highly successful biology professor. Her research was well known, so she was invited to give lectures all over the continent. Public speaking was her most important way to make positive use of an extraverted personality. Her lecturing style was described by others as at once riveting, sincere, and amusing.

Gloria grew up in a lower middle class family; neither of her parents had a university education. She was an unusually intelligent, lively, and engaging child, even though her mother often told her she was a handful. Gloria never had a warm relationship with her mother, whom she experienced as cold and critical. In a crucial incident that occurred when she was 10, Gloria experienced severe abdominal pain for several days but was told by her mother that it was not serious and that she should bear the discomfort. As a consequence of this neglect, her appendix burst and she developed peritonitis. The resultant adhesions made her sterile, which condition eventually became one factor leading to the breakdown of her marriage.

Gloria had a very different relationship with her father. They were not close in the sense of sharing intimate thoughts. Although her father, like her mother, failed to show her much physical affection, Gloria idealized and admired him from a distance, hoping to impress him with her achievements. Since she was naturally intelligent, she was able to succeed brilliantly in school and to rise out of her family's station in the lower middle class. Her younger brother, though his mother's favorite, was much less ambitious.

When Gloria was 18, she met her future husband, Michael, at the university. Their relationship was always highly intellectual. They could spend hours together playing complicated word games. Michael, who became a successful and well-paid lawyer, was a hero for Gloria. She enjoyed looking up to him and they lived in high style, buying the best furniture, eating the best food, and traveling all over the world.

The problem in their marriage involved competition. Michael liked Gloria best when she was one rung below him. When Gloria began to become successful in her own right, he withdrew from her. In addition, he wanted a child, which Gloria could not give him. When Michael left her, he quickly married a younger woman who provided him with a son and daughter. The dénouement of Gloria's marriage left her feeling that she would never be able to please any man.

After her divorce, Gloria had many lovers. She expressed surprise to the therapist that so many men, even married men, came on to her. She could not see that she did anything to encourage this behavior. In the observation of the therapist, she was not overtly flirtatious. Rather, she presented herself to men as a person of rare fascination. In Gloria's company, they seemed to find a whole dimension of life they had previously missed.

Gloria had several affairs while traveling to international conferences. She had many rendezvous with her lovers at meetings in far-off romantic cities. The men she met at home seemed much less satisfactory. For example, one of her fellow professors was highly attentive, but his dog-like devotion bored and irritated her. She admitted to the therapist that she was still looking for a man to put on a pedestal.

On one of Gloria's international excursions she met Nu, a Burmese diplomat working for the United Nations. Nu was much older than Gloria and extremely rich, and he had already been married three times. He swept Gloria off her feet and bought an expensive condominium for her, in which she entertained him on frequent visits. What Gloria later learned, to her dismay, was that Nu had several other women around the world with whom he had similar arrangements. Although his schedule was complicated, he somehow managed to fit everyone in. In spite of Nu's protestations that he really loved her best, Gloria was too proud to accept such a situation and their relationship came to an end.

Therapy

Suitability for Treatment

Gloria had functioned well in her career. She was a loyal friend and had maintained a commitment to her marriage for many years. This history suggested that she could persist at the tasks of therapy and benefit from an extended period of treatment.

Alliance and Structure

Gloria settled in to psychotherapy almost immediately. She enjoyed talking, and regaled the therapist with gossipy stories about well-known people. This behavior required persistent refocusing of her attention on the tasks of the treatment.

Modifying Histrionic Traits

Confrontations of Maladaptive Behaviors

Gloria's predominant problem was her feeling of rejection by significant men in her life. Her romanticism about the opposite sex had done little but create havoc. By searching for men to idealize, she consistently picked those who were highly narcissistic and therefore ultimately unable to care for her. When men did provide her with nurturance, she devalued them. As a result, the men who had the qualities she required were effectively excluded. In addition, her relationships with other women were overly competitive. Much of the work in the early months of treatment focused on these maladaptive behaviors.

The Psychodynamic Prong: Examining the Historical Context

The psychodynamic aspect of the treatment began with a discussion of Gloria's relationship with her parents. The therapist showed her how she had been hurt by her mother and frustrated by her father. She had tried to compensate for these emotional deficits by becoming endlessly brilliant and fascinating.

The Behavioral Prong: Development of Adaptive Alternatives

The cognitive-behavioral prong of the therapy concerned Gloria's maladaptive use of her personality traits. Thus, the therapist consistently challenged her romantic view of the world. In spite of being an academic, Gloria's reality consisted largely of impressions. She lived in technicolor, with hardly any grays in her world. In intimate relationships, her exaggerated extraversion was a problem. The therapist therefore encouraged her to be less colorful and more down to earth in her communicative style, keeping a focus on current issues in her life.

Making Better Use of Existing Traits

Gloria's personality was an asset in many ways. She was a superb lecturer as well as an ideal dinner companion. In small doses her company was intoxicating, but in large doses she lacked staying power. She was only able to turn off the "Gloria show" with her close female friends, from whom she obtained some degree of empathy and nurturance. The aim of the treatment was to help her use her extraversion when it was adaptive, but develop a more flexible strategy, primarily by becoming less dependent on obtaining a fix of attention from an admiring audience of men.

Outcome

Therapy helped Gloria see how her choices of intimate partners were destructive. Although the therapist suggested to her that she might be better off with someone more stable, Gloria insisted that she could not become attached to any man she could not look up to. It became clear that she was ambivalent about further intimacy, mainly because she was unwilling to risk further rejection. The therapist therefore helped her develop alternatives, largely through her attachments to nurturant female friends and maintaining a wide social network.

Close relationships reminded Gloria of her painful attachment to her highly neurotic mother. She therefore never regretted not having had children. Gloria needed, above all, to be free and a child would have dragged her down, preventing her from traveling and lecturing to her audiences. What worried her most was whether there would be anyone to look after her in her declining years.

At the end of the treatment, Gloria realized she could not handle the emotional dependency of a long-term intimate relationship and developed a lifestyle that provided her with some level of compensation for its absence. She accepted a single life but found lasting satisfaction through her work, particularly through her relationships to her students.

CASE EXAMPLE 2: CAROLE

History

Carole was a 22-year-old university student who presented for treatment after the breakup of a relationship with her lover. She had been seeing George for about a year, after having left her previous boyfriend, David, for him.

These two men represented two sides of a polarity. George was a charming and good-looking man who worked in his uncle's restaurant. In his relationship with Carole, he was quite inconsistent. Sometimes he would flatter her and make her feel like a million dollars. On other occasions he would ignore her or even publicly humiliate her. Her previous boyfriend, David, with whom she had gone out for several years, was a young engineer with a serious and devoted manner. Carole found him stable but boring. She was also extremely jealous of David's close relationship with his mother.

Carole was intensely interested in her physical appearance. She was a good-looking woman who loved to go out in the evening dressed to kill, so as to have men fawn over her. When she went to the gymnasium to keep up her shape, she laughingly observed that many of the men in the room were unable to concentrate on their own exercises. Her greatest pleasure was to walk into a room and to become the center of attention immediately. Women saw her as competitive, fearing that she might steal their boyfriends. As a result, she had few close friends of her own age, gravitating instead toward older women she could lean on.

Carole was a strong extravert. She spent little time at home and almost always had to be around people. In order to do her studies at the university, she would bring her books to cafés and, amidst the general din, write her papers there.

Carole had grown up in a working-class family. She had admired her parents and was shocked when their marriage ended. On later reflection, she realized that her parents had never shown much affection for each other and that her father, a small businessman, was hardly ever home. After the divorce, when Carole was 12, her mother worked in a small business with an uncle, but gradually slipped into alcoholism.

Carole had been an outgoing and engaging child. When, as a teenager, she had been thrown almost entirely on her own resources, her extraversion became amplified. Although she never really went wild, she discovered that she was attractive to the opposite sex. Eventually, being sexy took on the characteristics of an addiction.

Therapy

Suitability for Treatment

Carole had emerged from a difficult childhood and had been able to live on her own, support herself, and attend the university. She had many friends and most people found her engaging. All these qualities pointed to resourcefulness, a characteristic that bodes well for the success of psychotherapy.

Alliance and Structure

Carole enjoyed being a patient. The sessions usually began with a lively description of the latest dramatic incident in her life, accompanied by sarcastic commentaries on the deficiencies of other people. It took some effort on the therapist's part to get her to introspect. At first, she perceived these requests as disqualifying the validity of her complaints. Gradually, the therapist was able to show her that she avoided looking inside herself because doing so made her sad. She would often look plaintively at the therapist and ask, "Why do you want to make me cry?"

Modifying Histrionic Traits

Confrontations of Maladaptive Behaviors

Treatment focused on the consequences of Carole's excessive extraversion. The therapist pointed out that there were both good and bad aspects to this trait. On the one hand, she was naturally charming and genuinely enjoyed interacting with people. On the other hand, she was overly dependent on the reactions of others. Thus, she usually became angry and defensive when criticized. When she was ignored, she would escalate her attempts to get attention, sometimes to the point of putting herself in humiliating situations.

The Psychodynamic Prong: Examining the Historical Context

Carole had felt rejected by her narcissistic father and ignored by her alcoholic mother. Given her need for attention from other people, she had compensated for her deprivation by developing a charismatic personality. The problem was that whenever she felt left out of other people's lives, she re-experienced the sense of isolation she had felt as a child and struggled against ever since. The therapist communicated the idea that it was easier to understand her behavior in this context. Carole was acting out a drama with other people that ultimately related to her feelings of emotional deprivation from her parents.

The Behavioral Prong: Development of Adaptive Alternatives

Carole was encouraged to develop a greater capacity to be alone comfortably. She enjoyed reading, and learned to enjoy music without having to sit in a café. Carole had unusually high verbal skills and was majoring in languages. Although her own heritage was French, she had grown up in a Greek neighborhood and spoke that language like a native. She had the goal of developing an international business career.

Carole had several more unsuccessful relationships during the course of her treatment. Whenever she met a man who knew how to press her buttons, her thoughts were immediately covered by a romantic haze. She would often come to therapy describing some new relationship with enthusiasm. The therapist would usually suggest that it could be too early to tell whether the situation was favorable. He also encouraged her to learn how to develop a better checklist in choosing a man.

Carole believed in intuition and made most of her decisions on emotion. The therapist remarked that this approach had not been notably successful in the past and that she should consider modifying it. It was suggested to Carole that she should think of meeting men as a kind of job interview. One would not, after all, hire anyone without a resumé or references. Thus, although she need not ignore her initial feelings entirely, she was advised to check them out. Doing so should involve finding out about the man's track record with previous women. It would also involve taking other people's perceptions seriously. Thus, in several cases, Carole had been warned by her friends that the man she was seeing seemed to them to treat her inconsiderately. In the past, she would override this feedback, or, as often happened even when she felt angry at a man's behavior, she would let herself be sweet-talked out of a suitable response.

Making Adaptive Use of Existing Traits

Carole was an engaging woman with a wide social circle. However, much of her natural intelligence remained unused. One of the main goals of therapy, therefore, was to encourage her to take her university work more seriously. Success in this area would provide her with a grounding for her self-esteem that could be more stable than any heterosexual relationship. Carole eventually did well enough to gain admission to law school to prepare for an occupation in which dramatic behavior would be rewarded, without the dangers implicit in an intimate relationship.

Outcome

Therapy succeeded in helping Carole to stop choosing men with strong narcissistic traits and she was able to embark on healthier relationships. She became involved with Paul, an ambitious young lawyer, who was a steady, if less colorful, partner for Carole. Although, like everyone else, he found her lively and entertaining, he was also aware of her needy and vulnerable side. Paul was good at drawing her out and helping her deal with problems she had with other people in her life, most particularly her parents. Carole found that it was no longer necessary to live the life of a rich and famous person. She learned that when she felt supported emotionally, she no longer had the same need to maintain a high level of stimulation in her daily life.

SUMMARY

Some, but not all, histrionic patients successfully achieve intimacy. As discussed in the previous chapter, reasonable results in therapy do not necessarily require a Hollywood ending. Moreover, as pointed out by Storr (1988), psychotherapists have consistently overvalued intimate attachments while undervaluing solitude and separateness. There are ways other than romantic love to feel connected in life. This message is particularly important for patients with histrionic personality disorder.

8

Avoidant and Dependent Personality Disorders

To keep my mother in my room through the horrors of darkness ran too much counter to general requirements and to the wishes of others for such a concession as had been granted this evening to be anything but a rare and artificial exception. Tomorrow my anguish would return, and Maman would not stay by my side.
> —Marcel Proust, on anxious attachment

The next two chapters examine personality disorders characterized by anxious traits. Within a normal range, anxiety is an adaptive response to many environmental challenges. After all, our lives are rarely manageable without some level of vigilance and control. However, anxious traits become maladaptive when they interfere with social competence.

In contrast to those in the impulsive cluster, avoidant and dependent patients do not deal with anxiety by acting out. Instead, they withdraw from relationships unless assured of absolute safety, or look for protectors who can shield them from anxiety.

Avoidant personality disorder (APD) is characterized by hypersensitivity to rejection leading to withdrawal from intimate relationships. This diagnosis is very common in clinical practice (Oldham et al. 1995). It has also been found to be prevalent among psychiatric patients in cultures around the world (Loranger et al. 1994). The *DSM-IV* definition of APD requires the presence of at least four of the following seven criteria: avoidance of interpersonal contacts at work; unwillingness to get involved with people unless certain of being liked; restraint in intimate relationships; preoccupation with criticism and rejection; inhibition in new interpersonal situations; view of self as inept, unappealing or inferior; reluctance to take risks or engage in new activities.

Dependent personality disorder (DPD) is also seen in clinical practice (Hirschfeld et al. 1991). It is mainly characterized by a subordination of personal needs, making others assume responsibility for decisions, and by a lack of self-confidence (Bornstein 1992). The *DSM-IV* definition of DPD requires the presence of at least five of the following criteria: difficulty making decisions, need for others to assume responsibility, difficulty expressing disagreement, difficulty in initiation of projects, going to excessive lengths to obtain nurturance and support, feeling uncomfortable when alone, urgent need for replacement when close relationships end, and preoccupation with fears of being left alone. Although *DSM-IV* states that DPD is more common in women, other evidence (Bornstein 1992) suggests that this condition is equally common in men.

In their phenomenology, APD and DPD have many points of overlap. Moreover, studies examining demographics, comorbidity, family history, diagnostic sensitivity, or the specificity of traits to diagnoses, all show only minor differences between these two categories (Oldham et al. 1992, Reich 1990). Therefore, the present chapter will discuss these two conditions together, placing somewhat more emphasis on the more commonly seen avoidant category.

RELATIONSHIPS BETWEEN ANXIOUS TRAITS AND DISORDERS

Widiger and colleagues (1994), applying the Five Factor Model of personality, have described how patients in these categories differ in their personality traits from normal populations. Avoidant patients are high in introversion and high in neuroticism. Dependent patients are also high in neuroticism, but differ in being equally high on the dimension of agreeableness.

There has been very little research on the causes of avoidant or dependent personality disorders. Children can be born with an anxious temperament, causing them to respond to strangers or to other new situations with inordinate levels of fear. Yet with wise parental management, these traits can disappear over time. Kagan (1994) found this to be the case for about one-third of children with traits of behavioral inhibition, even though all the infants recruited into his study had originally been selected for research because of severe anxiety. The other two-thirds of his cohort remained fearful well into adolescence. With further follow-up, we may find that many of these individuals will tend to develop anxious symptomatology, such as generalized anxiety disorder and social phobia, as well as anxious cluster personality disorders.

Kagan found that parental practices make a great difference in the long-term outcome of behavioral inhibition in children. This observation follows clinical observations of overprotection (Levy 1943). Both psychoanalysts and behavioral therapists have long recognized that irrational anxiety benefits from exposure to feared situations. Thus, parents who go out of their way to expose a fearful child to social situations are most likely to produce recovery. Parents who respond overprotectively to the same behaviors will see them persist. These principles are confirmed by empirical research, and patients with dependent personality disorder consistently describe their parents as unusually overprotective (Baker et al. 1992, Head et al. 1991).

There are two mechanisms by which families can amplify anxious traits in children. The first is overprotection. The second, as suggested by Bowlby (1973), is modeling, by parents who are themselves fearful. Researchers (e.g., Fonagy et al. 1996) have actively investigated mechanisms involving a hypothesis that has been termed *intergenerational transmission* of anxious attachment. It is not clear whether parental behavior is the only factor determining transmission. It is also possible, as has been well documented for impulsivity (Zanarini 1993), that parents and children are similar largely because they share the same heritable personality traits. Moreover, parenting practices are themselves dependent on personality traits and are therefore under partial genetic control (Kendler 1996).

In summary, avoidant and dependent traits tend to be amplified by environments that reinforce them rather than extinguish them. Children who are constitutionally vulnerable to become anxious in social situations become more anxious when stressed, particularly if the stressors are continuous. Beyond a certain point, this process of amplification is difficult to reverse.

WORKING WITH ANXIOUS TEMPERAMENT

It follows from the above discussion that psychotherapy for an anxious temperament has to help patients face fear. As discussed in Chapter 4, patients with anxious personality structures run the risk of using therapy not as a place to learn new skills but as a place to hide. This is why a purely psychodynamic framework, focusing primarily on interpretations, can sometimes run into serious difficulties in this group. Patients may be happy to please the therapist by exploring the past as long as they are not required to change in the present. Therapists who believe that real change cannot take place until the patient has thoroughly worked through past experiences can be led down a garden path.

The psychodynamic and cognitive-behavioral prongs of therapy each play a role in treatment. The historical aspect of therapy can sometimes be helpful in convincing patients of the irrationality of fears. If, for example, there have been major losses and rejections in the patient's past, the therapist can point out how these experiences have been generalized.

The behavioral aspect of therapy is probably the most crucial aspect when working with anxious temperament. There has been no research on long-term therapy for anxious cluster disorders and only two formal studies of the treatment of avoidant personality (Alden 1989, Stravynski et al. 1994). Both showed that patients with APD can be helped by social skills training, a behavioral method encouraging them to overcome their anxiety and to learn new skills in dealing with people.

Dynamic therapists need to adopt some of these behavioral techniques to overcome the characterological resistance associated with avoidant or dependent personality structures. Without the learning of new skills, anxiety tends to feed on itself. The art of psychotherapy with anxious cluster patients lies in finding ways to encourage exposure to new situations.

In the examples to follow, we will look at two cases of avoidant personality disorder. Dynamically, neglect was the major factor in the first, and overprotection was crucial for the second. However, in both cases, the therapist's primary task was to address avoidant behavior and help the patient find ways to emerge from a highly constricted world view.

CASE EXAMPLE 1: CAMILLE

History

Camille was a 40-year-old family doctor who presented for treatment because of sad and lonely feelings. She had never married, nor had she ever been able to live with another person in an intimate relationship. The problem was that she was mortally afraid of rejection but felt intolerably confined by intimacy. Camille usually preferred to leave people before she could be left.

Camille was the last-born of seven children in a large French Catholic family. After her birth, her mother, who was already overburdened, suffered from a postpartum depression. As a result, Camille was sent to live with her aunt and uncle in a nearby town. She remembered these early years as happy. Her aunt, who had no children of her own, doted on her. Camille considered her aunt her primary caretaker and she had little contact with her parents and siblings.

This idyll came to an end when Camille's aunt developed cancer and died. Since her uncle was unable to care for a 6-year-old child, Camille was returned to her parents. In her new family situation, she felt neglected by both her parents and deeply resented by her older siblings. Camille had always been quite a shy child, and she made few friends. Since she was bright, she could compensate for the lack of affection in her family by doing well in school, becoming the favorite of the nuns, who were her beloved teachers.

As an adolescent, Camille thought of becoming a nun herself but decided she could serve others best by going into medicine. She excelled at her studies and eventually rose to a position of professional responsibility. Yet Camille had great difficulty establishing intimacy in her life. She did not date at all until she was out of medical school. She did not have a love affair until she was nearly 30. Her main source of intimacy was relationships with close female friends.

Her first serious relationship with a man began on the ski slopes. Lucien was a charming man who romanced her and made her feel attractive for the first time. He was ten years older than Camille and lived in a distant city, where he was unhappily married to a wife whom he was not willing to leave. In many ways, this situation suited Camille, who would have been too frightened to enter into a serious commitment. Thus, this affair lasted for the next ten years. Yet over time, Camille found herself feeling more and more angry with her lover. Things reached a point at which she could barely tolerate his visits. Camille was angry with Lucien when he arrived and angry when he left, and there was little time between arrival and departure to enjoy the relationship.

Therapy

Suitability for Treatment

Camille was a highly competent worker who also had loyal friends. Her difficulties were limited to the sphere of heterosexual intimacy. This picture suggested that she would be a good candidate for psychotherapy.

Alliance and Structure

Camille liked coming to therapy. She attended sessions faithfully, praising the therapist to her friends. Camille was excited at the opportunity to describe her deepest thoughts to another person, and often presented the therapist with complex and meaningful dream material. The therapist experienced her as engaging but clinging. Camille cried constantly throughout each session, and her habit of using half a box of tissues in each session made the therapist question his usual practice of providing a supply for his patients. It always seemed painful for Camille to end a session, and she often left the office as if she had just been condemned to imminent execution.

Working with Anxious Temperament

Confrontations of Maladaptive Behaviors

In spite of her fear of intimacy, Camille craved secure attachments. As a result, she was locked into an eternally ambivalent struggle with anyone who came close to her. This was most dramatically demonstrated by her relationship with Lucien. He would never leave his wife and, even if he did, she would not have been able to live with him. The therapist pointed out how these conflicts made her life unsatisfying.

The Psychodynamic Prong: Examining the Historical Context

The psychodynamic aspect of the therapy focused on Camille's early life experiences. The therapist pointed out how her interpersonal problems in the present reflected difficulties in establishing secure attachments in her family during childhood. Camille had experienced so many rejections and losses in the first few years of her life that, from then on, she became vigilant in order to defend herself against a repetition of these events. Camille's life had a secret agenda—to avoid dangerous attachments.

The Behavioral Prong: Development of Adaptive Alternatives

The behavioral aspect of the therapy focused on how these conflicts played themselves out in Camille's present life. She ended her relationship with Lucien but had few intimate relationships with men for a long time thereafter. Camille humorously reflected that since her relationships with women were much more sustaining, it was unfortunate that she did not have the capacity to become homosexual. Actually, it was the absence of physical intimacy that allowed Camille to be a loyal friend.

After a year of treatment, Camille was able to start a new relationship with Gil, a man she had met while visiting her accountant. Gil was divorced, and he was suitable for Camille in that he wanted a relationship but needed space. Nonetheless, the main problems between them were related to boundaries. Things usually went well if they saw each other on the weekend and called a few times during the week. At one point, when they actually tried to live together, they nearly broke up. When they returned to their previous arrangement, the relationship became reasonably successful.

Making Better Use of Existing Traits

Camille's anxious traits made her a rather cautious woman. She also had a fair number of compulsive traits and a strong need to control her environment. Her personality was adaptive for working as a physician, a task that required her to investigate complex clinical problems. In the course of therapy, Camille was able to find more satisfaction in her career. She had been working for many years at the same clinic and her co-workers had become like family to her. In this milieu, she could obtain validation without sacrificing space.

Outcome

Camille remained successful at work, and on follow-up she described herself as reasonably content with her life although she was still intermittently lonely. Developing as much closeness as she could handle allowed her to break the previous cycle that had led to so much distress. She learned that she no longer had to avoid rejection at the price of depriving herself of basic needs.

CASE EXAMPLE 2: JOANNE

History

Joanne was a 24-year-old law student who presented for therapy after being admitted to the hospital for a suicide attempt.

Joanne had grown up in an immigrant family in another city. She experienced her parents as highly overprotective and insensitive. She had been a shy and awkward child who had always had trouble making friends. She excelled at school, and her parents always gave her the impression that this was sufficient success for them. They tolerated little opposition to their wishes and used generous gifts to buy her compliance. She never discussed her inner feelings with her mother, who might feel personally threatened by any sign of discontent in her daughter.

Joanne was a studious adolescent who had little experience with the opposite sex. In spite of reasonably good looks, she always felt ugly. She was slightly overweight, largely because she used food for emotional comfort. Joanne became obsessed with the thought that her weight was the cause of her lack of social popularity. By the age of 18, she had developed secret and severe bulimic symptoms.

After finishing her undergraduate degree, Joanne realized

that her life was not on track. She felt that if she could just move away from home, everything would be all right. Over vociferous objections from her parents, she applied to universities out of town. When she was accepted to law school in a distant city, she was full of enthusiasm, ready to start a new life.

Not surprisingly, Joanne experienced many of the same problems in her new locale. Still a star student and now active in the student organization, Joanne kept herself extremely busy so as not to be lonely. However, she made few intimate friends and lacked any real success with the opposite sex. Joanne found it difficult to tolerate the uncertainty of the early stages of dating. She needed to know right away whether the relationship would be a stable one. Men saw her as clinging and tended to shy away.

Because she lacked consistent emotional support, Joanne's bulimia grew worse. The last straw occurred when her roommates asked her to leave because of her irregular eating behavior. Within a few days, she took an overdose of pills and was hospitalized.

Therapy

Suitability for Treatment

Joanne had managed to function at a high level in her studies. Her difficulties were focused on friendship and intimacy. There was therefore every reason to expect she could benefit from psychotherapy.

Alliance and Structure

Joanne developed a good working alliance. She became attached to the therapist but did not cling to him. She attended sessions regularly and never wallowed in her emotions. Her goal was to overcome the setbacks of the past year and re-establish her budding independence.

Working with an Anxious Temperament

Confrontations of Maladaptive Behaviors

The therapist pointed out how Joanne dealt with her anxiety by consistent avoidance. In hoping for a magical rescue either through leaving home or by finding a perfect lover, she had failed to learn the skills needed to become autonomous. The balance between her emotional needs and independence had been difficult to achieve. In order to stand on her own feet, she would also have to feel comfortable with her dependency. In practice, this would involve presenting herself to other people in a real way rather than simply impressing them with her accomplishments.

The Psychodynamic Prong: Examining the Historical Context

The psychodynamic aspect of therapy focused on the effects of growing up in a highly enmeshed family. Joanne had been overprotected by her parents, who actively resisted her attempts at separation. They had always expected her to put her family first. This prevented Joanne from having the quality of relationships with her peers during childhood and adolescence that would have helped prepare her for autonomous adult functioning. Moreover, her parents had always expected her to be a perfect daughter who would validate their own lives. As a result, they had failed to deal with Joanne's inner feelings. The therapist pointed out how she generalized these experiences, perceiving other people as expecting her to be perfect, in both mind and body, and not expecting them to provide her with minimal levels of understanding and empathy.

The Behavioral Prong: Development of Adaptive Alternatives

The behavioral aspect of therapy focused on Joanne's lack of social skills. She tended to be anxious and awkward outside of highly structured settings, such as her school. The therapist pointed out how her avoidance of situations that might conceivably lead either to friendship or to intimacy left her emotionally hungry inside, amplifying her bulimia.

Joanne felt that if she could not appear perfect to others, she would have to hide away. The clearest expression of this difficulty was her feeling about being mildly overweight. As her bulimia became less severe, she reached a set point that was stable, even though she had to accept that she did not look anything like a model.

Several of her friends were getting engaged and married. Joanne had three difficulties with attending these parties: her social awkwardness, her lack of a partner of her own, and her recent weight gain. It was a great achievement for her to force herself to go anyway. In addition to Joanne's mastery of her avoidant behavior, the achievement had a deeper significance: she was presenting her true self to the world as opposed to the false self that had been so encouraged by her family.

At the same time, Joanne experimented with other behaviors: opening up to a few old friends and dating men with the sole aim of having a pleasant evening. She was able to return to school for the next term and create a better balance in her life between outward performance and inner comfort.

Making Better Use of Existing Traits

Joanne might always suffer from social awkwardness, but she need not remain lonely. What helped her most was being in a structured environment. The more predictable the situation, the easier she found it to overcome her anxiety. For example, her activity in student government provided her with a safe haven, in which missteps would not lead to serious consequences.

As Joanne separated from her family, she was also able to build a better social network. She was gradually able to accept that her friends would not always have time for her, and learned not to feel devastated when she failed to be another person's priority.

Outcome

On two-year follow-up, Joanne was working in a corporate law firm. She had never been sufficiently extraverted to think of doing trial work. Instead, she found a niche in a job that involved careful research and quiet meditation. She was no longer bulimic, and she thought of her suicidality as a dark portion of her past to which she could never return.

SUMMARY

Avoidant and dependent personality disorders present special difficulties for psychotherapists. Not all patients respond to therapy. The main reason is that people with anxious temperaments find behavioral change anxiety-provoking. Therefore, working with these traits requires a combination of psychodynamic understanding and active behavioral interventions. The lesson is that insight need not always precede action. Just as often, action can lead to insight.

9

Compulsive Personality Disorder

"That's only a rough draft. Once I've succeeded in rendering perfectly the picture in my mind's eye, the rest will come easily." But before that, he admitted, there was lots of hard work to be done. He'd never dream of handing that sentence to a publisher in its present form.

—Albert Camus, on a writer who
has spent twenty years composing
the first sentence of his novel

Compulsive personality disorder (CPD) is characterized by emotional constriction, stubbornness, and rigidity. The clinical features of CPD center on the need for control in both work and interpersonal relationships. The *DSM-IV* definition of *obsessive-compulsive personality disorder* requires the presence of at least four of the following criteria: preoccupation with detail, perfectionism, excessive devotion to work, overconscientiousness, hoarding, reluctance to delegate tasks, miserliness, rigidity, and stubbornness.

COMPULSIVE TRAITS AND COMPULSIVE PERSONALITY

Applying the Five Factor Model of personality, Widiger and colleagues (1994) describe compulsive patients as high in neu-

roticism, low in agreeableness, and high in conscientiousness. Of
these, the trait most specifically related to compulsive personality is a high level of conscientiousness. In spite of their
differing approaches to therapy, Salzman (1968), Beck and
Freeman (1990), and Benjamin (1993) all place emphasis on the
importance of modifying perfectionistic and unreasonable expectations.

In many ways, conscientiousness is the converse of impulsivity (Widiger et al. 1994). The cognitive style of the compulsive is
also a mirror image of that seen in histrionic patients (Shapiro
1965). Instead of responding to emotions and drawing rapid
conclusions from general impressions, the compulsive depends
on thought and abstract reasoning, is greatly concerned with
details, and comes to conclusions very slowly.

Some children are naturally more conscientious than others.
In Livesley and colleagues's (1993) study of pathological traits in
normal twins, compulsivity had a heritability of nearly 40
percent.

What environmental factors can amplify compulsive traits to
pathological proportions? In the absence of research data, we are
forced to speculate. The discussion will therefore draw largely on
the clinical literature and the author's clinical experience with
compulsive patients.

As argued throughout this book, family patterns need not
be specific to any particular category of personality disorder.
Rather, the same stressful circumstances that can lead to
impulsive cluster disorders or to other anxious cluster disorders
could also amplify pre-existing compulsive traits. However, highly
compulsive children often have received inadequate levels of praise
and approval from their parents.

A conscientious child may respond to inadequate parental
validation by becoming even more conscientious. This mechanism might serve four psychological functions. First, the child
may be attempting to gain love by being good, as proposed by
Klein (1946) in her concept of a *depressive position*. Second, if
the parents are themselves compulsive, they are likely to be

critical of the child, who then must always try ever harder to please them. Third, diligently focusing on task performance can distract a child from troubling emotional problems. Fourth, most children learn that there are important rewards for conscientiousness, not only from their parents but also from other attachment figures, most particularly their teachers.

Conscientiousness, when sufficiently amplified, turns into perfectionism. No one can ever be quite sure that any task has been completed adequately. When emotional security depends entirely on external rewards, anxiety levels increase, further feeding doubts about the adequacy of one's performance. Fear of criticism and the need to be perfect can lead to serious procrastination.

WORKING WITH COMPULSIVITY

Therapy with compulsive patients can be tedious. The emotional range of the session is limited. The content is repetitive. The patient is rigid and unresponsive to feedback.

The problems described in the previous chapter concerning anxious cluster patients in therapy also apply to compulsive personality. Compulsive patients can use psychotherapy as a place to hide. Many of them also have life patterns in which procrastination plays a major defensive role. They are therefore happy to learn that important decisions must be delayed, in keeping with the hope that therapy will make them perfect, in which case they will be ready to make all the right choices. They are also attracted to the compulsive and rule-bound nature of psychotherapy. It is comforting to come always at the same time, to talk always of the same things, and to hear the therapist's predictable comments. Most of all, compulsive patients fear making a mistake. They become anxious if they have to give up control of any aspect of their lives to another person. This is why they can strenuously resist active pressure for change.

Yet in many ways, psychotherapy is easier when the patient has compulsive traits. There is a great deal to be said for patients who come to their sessions, and who, when angry, do not abandon the treatment. Changes may be slow, but when they happen, they are more likely to stick.

Much of the therapeutic work with compulsive patients involves modifying perfectionistic expectations. Again, therapy has two prongs. The first prong is historical, showing the patient how a normally conscientious approach to life became exaggerated in response to an unyielding and unsupportive family environment.

The second prong involves changing behavior in occupational and interpersonal spheres. By lowering expectations of themselves, and by modifying perfectionistic standards of task completion, compulsive patients can reduce procrastination. At the same time, they can learn to be less rigid and demanding with colleagues and subordinates.

Some of the most difficult work with compulsive patients involves improving their intimate relationships. Some patients will avoid intimacy entirely, while others will become phobic the moment issues of commitment come up. The rationalization for avoiding commitment can be, "Why should I settle for this person when I might find someone better?" The dilemma of the compulsive is that the fear of choice leads them to end up having nothing at all.

When individuals with compulsive personality traits choose partners, they may be attracted to their opposite. Research shows that most people's marital choices are based on similarity (Mascie-Taylor 1989). However, attraction to a partner is also based on the complementarity of character (Dicks 1967). Thus, it is not unusual to see a couple in which one partner (usually the man) is compulsive, while the other (usually the woman) has histrionic traits. This pairing is well known to couple therapists (Jacobsen and Gurman 1995), since it creates a pattern in which the histrionic partner becomes the pursuer and the compulsive partner the pursued. In systemic terms, one partner is pressing for higher levels of interaction while the other is working to keep levels lower.

Compulsive individuals are attracted to histrionic partners because they make them feel more excited and alive. At the same time, the histrionic individuals may be attracted to compulsive partners because they provide needed stability. Over time, disappointment may arise on both sides. The compulsive partner finds the histrionic overdemanding. The histrionic finds the compulsive partner rigid and ungiving. In the end, the couple can bring out the worst in each other. To break this cycle, the compulsive patient needs to learn to see the partner's needs as valid, and also to see that when one validates other people, they usually become less demanding.

Compulsive individuals need not always be attracted to histrionic partners. If both people in a relationship have strong compulsive traits, a different set of difficulties arises, usually involving a power struggle in which both sides vie for control.

As will be demonstrated in the case examples, compulsivity tends to be more functional in work and less functional in intimate relationships. As with other categories of personality disorders, much of the work of therapy involves helping the patient to handle intimacy.

CASE EXAMPLE 1: JEAN-PIERRE

History

Jean-Pierre, a 47-year-old businessman, presented for therapy after the failure of his second marriage. His wife of ten years, after beginning an extramarital affair, summarily locked him out of their house and informed him that their relationship was over.

Jean-Pierre had come from an upwardly mobile family, his parents having emigrated from France to Canada before the Second World War. His father had obtained a position in the provincial government but the family had always faced a difficult financial struggle. This situation became markedly worse after the sudden death of his father when Jean-Pierre was 15, which left his mother a widow with three children.

Jean-Pierre was an unusually intelligent young man. With the help of loans, he was able to get through business school with little effort, and he even obtained a scholarship to spend a post-graduate year at Harvard, where, as he described it, he was able to hold his own with "the best and the brightest." After his return, he obtained a job with a good firm. Although initially considered a comer, he never came close to being considered for a partnership.

When he was 26, Jean-Pierre married Valerie, a hardworking woman from a middle-class family whom he met at work. She stayed home after the birth of their two daughters, who were left almost entirely in their mother's care. Jean-Pierre gradually began to feel that his wife was dull. He craved the excitement he had missed as a young man, when he was too busy working his way through university to sow any wild oats.

Jean-Pierre also felt that his wife was insufficiently attentive to him. Over time, his feelings started to border on contempt. Valerie was often ill, exhausted from raising her two children with very little help. Once, when Jean-Pierre invited clients to their home, she burned the dinner. Instead of seeing this as a sign of stress reflecting a need for support, he saw her as incompetent.

When he was 35, Jean-Pierre met Denise, who became the great obsessive love of his life. Denise was a successful lawyer a few years younger than he, highly attractive to men and from a very wealthy family. She had previously had a long series of affairs with married men and this was her latest conquest. Jean-Pierre stated that he felt alive for the first time. He had married a woman as compulsive as himself, but with Denise, life was entertaining, almost cinematic.

Jean-Pierre soon divorced Valerie and married Denise. The couple did almost everything together. They lunched together every day at work and spent the entire weekend in each other's company. Their sex life stayed at a high level because Denise demanded intercourse several times a day and was strongly interested in reaching orgasm. The large inheritance that Denise brought to the marriage allowed them to live in great style, traveling first class all over the world.

Denise had no desire for children of her own and resented having Jean-Pierre's daughters visit them. Jean-Pierre was upset by this situation but thought that whatever he had lost by ending his first marriage would be more than compensated for by the magic of his love for Denise. During the years of their marriage, as he concentrated all his energy on this relationship, his career stagnated.

Jean-Pierre was faithful to Denise, but the marriage, though initially exciting, became increasingly boring. His wife's constant need for attention wore Jean-Pierre down and he found himself needing more space. As he gradually began to withdraw from Denise, she retaliated, first with a series of flirtations, then with flagrant extramarital affairs, finally leaving him for a man she had hired to redo her basement.

Therapy

Suitability for Treatment

Jean-Pierre's treatability was indicated by his ego strengths, as demonstrated by a history of having persisted in life tasks both in work and in close relationships.

Alliance and Structure

Jean-Pierre's relationship to his therapist might best be described as collegial. He talked in his normal way, which was pretentious, intellectual, and patronizing. (He was surprised that both his co-workers and the women in his life perceived him as condescending.) This trait did not prevent Jean-Pierre from forming an alliance with the therapist, which he saw as necessary to make sense of what had happened to him. Jean-Pierre was not a man of deep emotion, but he was able to acknowledge that he had overestimated his own capacity to judge other people and had behaved "like an ass."

Modifying Compulsivity

Confrontations of Maladaptive Behaviors

Therapy aimed to help Jean-Pierre reduce his unrealistic expectations of himself. His compulsivity had prevented him from accomplishing what he might have been capable of at work. He was tempted to rationalize these failures, bitterly reflecting on how other, less competent people had been promoted when he had not. The therapist encouraged him to take more responsibility for his underachievement and to look for ways through which he could still develop.

Jean-Pierre's compulsivity had also interfered with his developing a social network. He had few friends of his own, having centered his life almost entirely on Denise and her circle. Moreover, his defensive arrogance led him to devalue other people's accomplishments and talents. With more reasonable expectations of himself, he could become more tolerant of others and develop more flexible strategies for attachment.

Inevitably, the main subject of the sessions was Jean-Pierre's relationship with Denise. The majority of the interventions by the therapist consisted of confrontations concerning the irrational nature of this attachment. The therapist described the marriage as a magic theatre, an illusion inside which Jean-Pierre attempted to return to his adolescence. In doing so, he was avoiding other important issues, most particularly his productivity and his responsibilities to his children. Although this relationship provided short-term satisfactions, acceding to the wishes of a histrionic woman left him feeling emotionally empty in the long run.

The Psychodynamic Prong: Examining the Historical Context

The therapist pointed out to Jean-Pierre that he had attempted to compensate for the aridity of his childhood through the attachment to Denise. Valerie, like his mother, was a burdened woman who failed to provide him with real emotional satisfaction. Ultimately, his attempt to find happiness through remarriage had failed because no other person could provide him what he lacked within himself.

The Behavioral Prong: Development of Adaptive Alternatives

Jean-Pierre responded to the therapist's confrontations. He was already well into middle age, by which time his dreams had been tamed by a series of disappointments and reverses. His sense of limited time in life helped the treatment to move rather quickly. Within a few weeks after Denise left him, he embarked on a new relationship with Suzanne, a divorced woman working in his firm. Although the therapist was doubtful about the timing, Jean-Pierre's new attachment proved a success.

Suzanne lacked both the sexual magnetism and the destructive narcissism that had characterized Denise. She was a practical person who was not particularly glamorous. Jean-Pierre found that this new relationship grounded him in a way that his second marriage had not.

He also worked in therapy on his jealousy of Suzanne's attachment to her 15-year-old son Peter. Jean-Pierre's over-controlling and condescending manner proved disastrous with an adolescent and enraged Suzanne. Eventually, he came to realize that he had to define what he could and could not control in his environment. In coming to this insight, he realized that Suzanne had many of the same good qualities as Valerie, whose value Jean-Pierre was now able to perceive.

Jean-Pierre accepted that he had sacrificed his wife and children for a chimera. Valerie had long since remarried, but he could still make meaningful amends to his two daughters. Although they were now grown women, they still needed a father in their lives.

Making Better Use of Existing Traits

Jean-Pierre's compulsivity was most useful in his work and he began to reconsider how he could salvage his career. Unable to meet his own standards, Jean-Pierre was also a serious disappointment to his partners. They expected much more of a man with a Harvard degree, although he had never been in danger of losing his job. His strongest card as a businessman was his passion for details, particularly those that escaped the notice of his partners. By modifying his expectations of himself and others, he was able to use his skills more productively.

Jean-Pierre had been equally exacting in his home environment. As he learned to know the things he could and could not change, his attention to detail became more of an asset. He obtained more gratitude from his mate by keeping a vigilant eye on the house with a view to its proper maintenance than he had ever obtained by hectoring others with sharp criticism. Even Peter warmed up when his mother's lover was not always on his case. Suzanne, a lively but rather disorganized woman, was grateful that she could depend on Jean-Pierre to keep track of her finances.

Outcome

Jean-Pierre transferred to a new department at his firm where he could train younger people. As a middle-aged man, he sought pleasure from generativity, no longer feeling that he had to conquer the world. His relationship with Suzanne and with his own children became more stable. Jean-Pierre arranged a series of ski holidays in which he, Suzanne, her son, and his daughters and their boyfriends could all spend meaningful time together.

*   *   *

This case demonstrates some of the classical dynamics of compulsive behavior. This patient was highly conscientious, but at midlife, he was unable to deal with his disappointment at not having met his unreasonably high expectations. Like many people with compulsive personality structure, he was strongly attracted to his mirror image, a histrionic woman. This relationship, which almost entirely lacked boundaries, proved destructive. In the course of the treatment, he was able to develop a different kind of attachment, grounded in mutuality and realism.

CASE EXAMPLE 2: JILL

History

Jill was a 25-year-old medical student. She presented for treatment because of disruptive anxiety that had developed when she started doing clinical work on hospital wards. She had experienced one clear-cut panic attack but most of her symptoms involved anticipatory anxiety. It became apparent that these feelings were linked to perfectionistic expectations.

Jill always needed to be perfect in every way—as a friend, as a doctor, as a lover, and as a beauty. Although she was admired by many men, they usually found her to be an inaccessible ice princess. As a result, she ended up feeling alone and unloved. In compensation, Jill became overly dedicated to her work and dealt with expectations in a rigid and overconscientious way.

Jill had grown up in a large Irish-Catholic family that was considered a model by their priest and their local community. She was the sixth born of seven, and her two brothers and four sisters were all unusually good-looking, hard-working, and successful.

Jill's father, though somewhat prone to excess drinking, made a good living for the family until he died of cancer when Jill was 16. Her mother, who had devoted herself to the raising of the children, was emotionally unsupportive. The father's death exaggerated a situation in which the children were already expected to fend for themselves.

Jill had tended to her father's needs as he lay dying in the hospital. (One of the situations that stirred up her anxiety in the course of her clinical work involved the catheterization of a cancer patient, which brought back many painful memories.)

Jill did not feel that she had been a favorite child. After all, her sisters were clever and beautiful young women. Their interactions with each other were often marked by bitingly critical comments focusing on minor imperfections of dress or conduct. Thus, Jill grew up in an environment in which there was little space to have a bad day and little opportunity to talk if one did happen to have one.

As an adolescent, Jill was conscientious in her studies, earning a scholarship to a prestigious and expensive women's college. She expected that her high school boyfriend, who decided to attend school at home, would wait for her return. When, after a few months, he dumped her rather unceremoniously, she was crushed. Yet instead of feeling angry, Jill assumed that she must be deficient. For several years afterwards, she avoided intimate relationships, concentrating on getting into medical school.

In her first year of medical training, Jill entered into a brief love affair with a fellow student. He was highly competitive and intellectual, and she described the relationship as a challenge. They spoke very little about intimate matters to each other. Instead they would spend hours quizzing each other about obscure bits of medical knowledge. After a few months, Jill found herself rejected.

Jill had been looking forward to working with patients as a way of proving her competence and her compassion. It came as a shock that she would respond to life-threatening illness emotionally. On one occasion she fled in panic from the room of an accident victim. Bedside teaching, in which senior physicians asked difficult and probing questions of the students, was particularly humiliating for her. Jill imagined that the other members of her group had no trouble with these situations and that her anxiety only proved her incompetence as a physician.

Therapy

Suitability for Treatment

Jill was high-functioning and hard-working, with many loyal friends. She was clearly an excellent candidate for psychotherapy.

Alliance and Structure

Jill had difficulty starting therapy sessions because she was so used to responding to cues from other people. She would begin by asking the therapist how *he* was and then anxiously demand that he ask her questions. In spite of these initial difficulties, once Jill got used to the process, she learned to sit down and talk quite readily. She came on time and almost never missed a session.

Managing Compulsivity

Confrontations of Maladaptive Behaviors

The therapist pointed out how Jill was grounding herself by orienting her responses to other people's expectations. She could never confide in anyone and could never be real. The therapist explained to her that just as doctors have to monitor input and output in patients, they cannot function in their own lives without balancing what they do for others and what they can get others to do for them.

The Psychodynamic Prong: Examining the Historical Context

The psychodynamic aspect of the therapy focused on Jill's experience growing up in her family. Even before the death of her father, her parents were overburdened and unable to respond to emotional needs in their children. Moreover, the siblings, instead of banding together, competed to gain the approval of parents who intensely wanted their children to rise in the world. Jill had responded to her isolation by focusing everything on her performance. As a result, every situation in which she could fail became a matter of life and death. She was reacting to medical school as to a critical and unempathic family.

The Behavioral Prong: Development of Adaptive Alternatives

Jill continued to feel anxious on the wards but was able to accept the therapist's advice to tolerate the feeling until she could master it. Jill needed deconditioning, whereby she could expose herself to situations in which she might face criticism and find that the consequences were less severe than she had anticipated.

Jill also began a new intimate relationship with one of her fellow students. Bashir, like Jill, had done most things in life on his own, but unlike her, he had always received enough family support to be able to take care of other people comfortably. Jill had the experience of leaning on someone for the first time. Once she felt protected by her relationship to Bashir, she could let her hair down and enjoy their time together. She had to make adjustments to being with an easygoing man who did not particularly care whether she was perfect. Thus, they sometimes quarreled over Bashir's lack of punctuality and his failure to compliment her on her choice of clothing. Nonetheless, she found that her increased capacity for enjoying herself usually provided sufficient compensation for these deficits.

Making Better Use of Existing Traits

Jill's compulsivity, however problematic, was also a potential asset. In her work, if she was no longer terrified of being wrong, she could become competent and build her self-esteem. Instead of worrying about her own competence, she could use her attention to detail for the benefit of patients and become a careful and knowledgeable professional.

Outcome

On one-year follow-up Jill was functioning well at work and in her relationship. Although each time she faced a new challenge at work she felt anxiety, she learned that these feelings did not have to be uncontrollable. By looking forward to unloading and having down time with Bashir, she felt less trapped by the demands of others.

SUMMARY

Compulsive patients suffer from rigidity and perfectionism. In both these case examples, patients were able to reduce trait amplification by developing more flexible strategies to deal with the demands of work and intimacy. Since many of us share compulsive characteristics with patients, we often know about these problems from our own experience. Like every other trait, compulsivity can either work for us or against us.

10
Summary and Conclusions

WORKING WITH TRAITS: A SUMMARY

We can now briefly review the main arguments of this book:

- Personality disorders develop when normal personality traits become amplified to a level at which they become maladaptive. This process depends on genetic factors (temperamental intensity) as well as on environmental factors (negative life experiences and conflicts between traits and social expectations).
- The treatment of personality disorders tends to be difficult. Traditional methods of psychotherapy, focusing on the exploration of childhood experiences, can run aground for lack of specific mechanisms for changing maladaptive behaviors. Patients with personality disorders need a two-pronged therapeutic approach that combines an understanding of life history based on psychodynamics with a technology for change based on cognitive-behavioral principles.
- The presence of a personality disorder is not, by itself, an indication for psychotherapy. Therefore, we need to apply therapeutic resources in a cost-effective way. The most suitable patients will usually have significant ego strengths along with moderate levels of dysfunction.

- Research shows that the most effective ingredient in any psychotherapy is a strong alliance with the therapist, providing a channel through which the treatment can address current life problems.
- Since personality traits are stable over time, therapists should not expect radical change in character structures.
- Patients with personality disorders need to learn to use their trait profiles in new ways. This process involves unlearning maladaptive behaviors as well as learning adaptive ones. The outcome should be a broad and flexible behavioral strategy.
- The main focus of therapy is the analysis of current life situations. Although historical background is important, understanding present difficulties always comes first.
- In each category of personality disorder, the therapeutic strategy depends on understanding underlying traits. In the impulsive cluster, the emphasis is on improving impulse control and learning how to manage dysphoric emotions. In the anxious cluster, the emphasis is on overcoming avoidance and excessive needs for control.

PERSONALITY AND THE LIMITS OF PSYCHOTHERAPY

One of the main messages of this book is that there are limits to the effectiveness of psychotherapy. The Introduction discussed how psychotherapists may follow the rules but still fail to obtain good results in their patients. We often respond to the inevitable frustrations of practice by blaming ourselves, either for inadequate training or lack of skill. We may feel that if only we were as clever and insightful as other therapists, our treatments would be consistently successful. These considerations lead us to seek consultations, attend conferences, and read books about psychotherapy. These are constructive responses, but we should not believe that when we fail to find answers to difficult clinical problems, there will always be someone else who can.

The treatment of personality disorders benefits from a broad model of their origins. Genetic factors play a major role in virtually every mental disorder and the personality disorders are no exception (Paris, in press). However, patients with personality disorders, unlike those with some mental disorders, do not just suffer from chemical imbalances. Personality disorders derive in part from unusually intense levels of traits, but they will not ordinarily develop without strong input from environmental factors.

Nevertheless, taking traits into account should help us stop unnecessarily banging our heads against the walls of psychopathology. As discussed in Chapters 1 and 2, personality traits have strong genetic roots. Thinking of personality as a biological given need not in any way produce nihilism or despair. Rather, as we have tried to show, biology is the ground on which behavior stands. Taking the terrain into account helps us go further. Subscribing to trait theory helps us to deal with much of the frustration we experience as practitioners of psychotherapy. Instead of blaming ourselves for not being sufficiently competent, we can focus on the intrinsic limits of psychotherapy, many of which are rooted in personality.

Therapists who go on seeing patients for years may be attempting to meet unreasonable goals. Patients vary in their intrinsic capacities to make use of treatment. As reviewed in Chapter 3, patients with low levels of previous functioning may fail to benefit from any form of psychotherapy. Patients with personality disorders have impairments in many functional areas. We need not offer treatments requiring large allocations of human resources to patients who cannot really use them. It makes the most sense to invest ourselves in patients who are competent in major sectors of their lives but maladaptive in other sectors, most usually in managing intimate relationships.

We also have to accept that the prospects for some patients remain constricted. If therapists set their goals lower and are ready to quit when they are ahead, they can be less frustrated. This is the rationale behind intermittent rather than continuous therapy (McGlashan 1993), which approach makes better use of our resources and is also much more in concordance with the chronicity of personality pathology.

Finally, we need to be more flexible and eclectic in our methods. The same form of treatment may not be suitable for patients with different levels of functioning. Moreover, we need different strategies for different categories of personality disorder. Methods that are suitable for impulsive disorders might not be appropriate for patients in the anxious cluster and vice versa. Therapists with a single approach are like tailors making only one size of suit.

HOW DO WE KNOW WHEN PSYCHOTHERAPY IS WORKING?

The longer the treatment, the more difficult it is to assess its progress. Many years ago, Roethlisberger and Dickson (1939) reported on the effect on productivity of various changes in the working environment of a factory in Hawthorne, New Jersey. They found that any change temporarily increased the productivity of the work force, but that no change produced more than a transient impact. This phenomenon, which has been termed the *Hawthorne effect* (Adair 1984) and resembles the well-known placebo effect in medicine, often goes unrecognized by therapists.

Let us consider an instructive example from the history of psychiatry. Years ago, clinicians working in the back wards of mental hospitals had many regressed psychotic patients under their care. The therapists were, understandably, willing to try almost anything that might conceivably help their patients. As a result, the literature of that time described all kinds of experimental treatments (Mora 1975). Patients were treated with frontal lobotomies (Valenstein 1986), insulin coma therapy, or massive doses of electroconvulsive therapy (Collins 1988). On the psychotherapeutic side, Rosen (1953) published a description of a dramatic technique he called "direct analysis."

Clinicians working with psychotic patients learned over time that almost any intensive intervention, even daily occupational therapy, that exposed patients to novel stimuli, produced transient positive effects. Careful follow-up studies of all these interventions, organic and psychotherapeutic, showed that improvements seen in the short-term were not sustained over time (Lehmann 1975). What we had been looking at was a series of Hawthorne effects.

With a better understanding of the psychoses, we can see more clearly why patients failed to respond to treatments current forty years ago. The strong genetic factors in these illnesses limited the success of all interventions. Even the antipsychotic drugs of today, though reasonably effective, only suppress symptoms rather than cure the underlying illness. We have also learned not to offer intensive psychotherapy to schizophrenic patients. Research has shown that the most effective psychological interventions in schizophrenic populations are psychoeducational and rehabilitative (Hogarty et al. 1991).

There are parallels between the history of the treatment of the psychoses and that of the personality disorders. In both cases, patients are difficult and frustrating for clinicians. Moreover, psychotherapeutic interventions in patients with personality disorders can yield a series of Hawthorne effects. Each time a new intervention is introduced, the patient seems to get better for a while and then regresses. A wit once called this process "cyclotherapy." Finally, since psychiatrists and family doctors tend to focus on Axis I symptoms and often ignore Axis II pathology, drugs are too often prescribed for personality-disordered patients. Again, medications seem to work for a few months and then mysteriously stop working.

In summary, patients in long-term treatment of any kind have their ups and downs. We cannot always know whether intensive treatments are working or whether the passage of time is helping patients to learn new skills. It is therefore not cost-effective to offer continuous treatment for all patients. My experience in using intermittent therapy has been that many patients come back six months or a year later, having made major changes in their lives. If they had been kept in therapy, it would have been tempting to conclude that their gains depended largely on the continuity of treatment.

In order to conceptualize how personality disorders might be reversed in therapy, we need to understand in much greater detail the mechanisms by which they develop. The next section of this chapter is devoted to suggesting guidelines for further research.

WORKING WITH TRAITS: GUIDELINES FOR RESEARCH

As a born-again convert to the principle of applying research findings to clinical practice, I believe that the field of psycho-therapy will not progress without a much stronger evidence base. Ultimately, recommendations for psychological treatments, like medical treatments, must be based on empirical studies of their efficacy. When our methods become rooted securely in data, they will not be radically different even when different people provide the service.

I have offered here a theoretical model that can account for the personality disorders. It must, however, remain theoretical until we have enough evidence to prove it true or false or at least to significantly modify it. I have also attempted to make some common-sense recommendations for the treatment of personality-disordered patients. However intuitively correct they seem, every one of these ideas needs to be tested.

Ideally, the treatment approach presented in this book would need to be organized in the form of a manual that anyone could use as a guide to conduct the therapy. (This does not mean that clinicians need to work from a manual, but rather that a structured description is a necessary precondition to investigat-ing the efficacy of treatment.) A large number of patients would be treated by well-trained therapists. A study could determine the effectiveness of treatment by comparing the outcomes of two different modes of therapy in two groups of patients with the same pathology.

It would be particularly important for researchers to evaluate a complete course of treatment. Most of the existing studies describe treatments of twenty sessions or fewer, with the longest courses running about a year. This is simply not an adequate time to assess the outcome of therapy for the personality disorders.

We must also study the outcome of treatment using a variety of measures. We usually need to know whether the patient has fewer symptoms, whether the patient is functioning better in work and in relationships, and whether the patient actually feels better inside. Finally, we must determine whether any positive outcomes achieved remain stable after treatment is terminated. This kind of follow-up data, which is crucial for disorders that are known to be chronic, is too often absent from the research literature.

Even the best studies on psychotherapy have failed to meet all the criteria described above. The proposed research will most probably not be carried out in the near future, since it requires major expenditures of human resources. Unless granting agencies become willing to increase their funding for psychotherapy research fairly dramatically, we have to continue to depend on clinical acumen.

However, we need not be discouraged about the value of such research. As shown here, the existing literature already has practical implications for clinical work. As researchers carry out more studies demonstrating the effectiveness of particular methods of treatment, we will continue to learn from their success, creating universal standards of care for evidence-based practice.

Most therapists reading this book will already have developed their own methods of approach to patients. They will not be looking to start from scratch. However, they will welcome ways to expand their repertoire of interventions. They should therefore pay attention to what may be the most crucial elements of those therapies that have empirically demonstrated their effectiveness.

Research on psychotherapy consistently shows that the most effective elements in treatment involve a strong therapeutic alliance, a trusting relationship with a therapist, and a powerful emotional experience. We might therefore be spending more time thinking about the quality of our relationships with our patients and less on the accuracy of our interventions.

Psychodynamic therapists can learn from their cognitive-behavioral colleagues. For example, Linehan's success with an unusually low-functioning group of patients with borderline personality disorder provides useful clues to therapists who are not behaviorists on how to control impulsivity. Similarly, if research confirms that social skills training is an effective procedure for patients with avoidant personality disorder, psychodynamic therapists should incorporate these methods into their repertoires.

A VISION OF THE FUTURE

I envision a future in which psychotherapy will have one universal form. Of course, psychotherapists themselves will never be interchangeable. Our own personality traits will make sure of that! Some of us work best in active dialogue. Others are more receptive and "holding." Both approaches can be effective.

Yet, a widely practiced, evidence-based, and eclectic method of therapy must arise out of the clamor and confusion of the present scene, with its multiple schools and its endless proliferation of theories and methods. This book has attempted to contribute to the process by melding the best elements of the psychodynamic and behavioral traditions.

The ideas in this book have not been presented as a new method of psychotherapy. In fact, most of what I have written here is not really that new. What I have attempted to do is integrate many different ideas from many different sources to create a jargon-free and pragmatic approach to treatment.

Experienced therapists know that when we understand a patient, we can communicate that understanding through the simplest words. In this sense, there is nothing mysterious about working with traits.

Perhaps the most important point that the reader can take from this book is that psychotherapists must respect individual differences. What works well for one patient may be entirely wrong for another. This is the main reason understanding personality traits is crucial for practice. However much we understand the mind, each person is unique. This is why every patient must take a different path to making life more liveable.

References

Adair, J. G. (1984). The Hawthorne effect: a reconsideration of the methodological artifact. *Journal of Applied Psychology* 69:334–345.

Adler, G. (1979). The myth of the therapeutic alliance in borderline patients. *American Journal of Psychiatry* 136:642–645.

——— (1985). *Borderline Psychopathology and Its Treatment*. New York: Jason Aronson.

Adler, G., and Myerson, P., eds. (1973). *Confrontation in Psychotherapy*. New York: Science House.

Alden, L. (1989). Short-term structured treatment for avoidant personality disorder. *Journal of Consulting and Clinical Psychology* 57:756–764.

Alexander, F., and French, T. (1946). *Psychoanalytic Therapy*. New York: Ronald.

American Psychiatric Association (1994). *Diagnostic and Statistical Manual of Mental Disorders, 4th Edition*. Washington, DC: American Psychiatric Press.

Andreoli, A., Frances, A., Gex-Fabry, M., et al. (1993). Crisis intervention in depressed patients with and without *DSM-III-R* personality disorders. *Journal of Nervous and Mental Disease* 181:732–736.

Andrews, G. A. (1991). Anxiety, personality, and the anxiety disorders. *International Review of Psychiatry* 3:293–302.

Arbel, N., and Stravynski, A. (1991). A retrospective study of separation in the development of adult avoidant personality disorder. *Acta Psychiatrica Scandinavica* 83:174–178.

Bair, D. (1995). *Anais Nin: A Biography*. New York: Putnam.

Baker, J. D., Capronn, E. W., and Azorlosa, J. (1996). Family environment characteristics of persons with histrionic and dependent personality disorders. *Journal of Personality Disorders* 10:82–87.

Baker, L. A., Cesa, I. L., Gatz, M., and Mellins, C. (1992). Genetic and environmental influences on positive and negative affect: support for a two-factor theory. *Psychology & Aging* 7:158–163.

Bandura, A. (1977). *Social Learning Theory*. Englewood Cliffs, NJ: Prentice Hall.

Beck, A. T., and Freeman, A. (1990). *Cognitive Therapy of Personality Disorders*. New York: Guilford.

Benjamin, J., Patterson, C., Greenberg, B. D., et al. (1996). Population and familial association between the D4 receptor gene and measures of novelty seeking. *Nature Genetics* 12:81–84.

Benjamin, L. (1993). *Interpersonal Diagnosis and Treatment of Personality Disorders: A Structural Approach*. New York: Guilford.

Bergeman, C. S., Chipuer, H. M., Plomin, R., et al. (1993). Genetic and environmental effects on openness to experience, agreeableness, and conscientiousness: an adoption/twin study. *Journal of Personality* 61:158–179.

Beutler, L. E., Machado, P. P., and Neufeldt, S. A. (1994). Therapist variables. In *Handbook of Psychotherapy and Behavior Change*, ed. A. E. Bergin and S. L. Garfield, pp. 229–269. New York: Wiley.

Black, D. W., Baumgard, C. H., and Bell, S. E. (1995). A 16–45 year follow-up of 71 men with antisocial personality disorder. *Comprehensive Psychiatry* 36:130–140.

Bond, M., Paris, J., and Zweig-Frank, H. (1994). Defense styles and borderline personality disorder. *Journal of Personality Disorders* 8:28–31.

Bond, M. P., Gardner, S., Christian, J., and Sigal, J. J. (1983). Empirical study of self-rated defense styles. *Archives of General Psychiatry* 40:333–338.

Bornstein, R. F. (1992). The dependent personality: developmental, social, and clinical perspectives. *Psychological Bulletin* 112:3–23.

Bowlby, J. (1973). *Attachment and Loss: Separation*. London: Hogarth.

Boyer, L., and Giovacchini, P. L., eds. (1990). *Master Clinicians on Treating the Regressed Patient*. Northvale, NJ: Jason Aronson.

Browne, A., and Finkelhor, D. (1986). Impact of child sexual abuse: a review of the literature. *Psychological Bulletin* 99:66–77.

Buckley, P., Karasu, T. B., and Charles, E. (1981). Psychotherapists view their personal therapy. *Psychotherapy* 18:299–305.

Burks, J., and Rubenstein, M. (1979). *Temperament Styles in Adult Interaction*. New York: Brunner/Mazel.

Camus, A. (1948). *The Plague*, trans. S. Gilbert. New York: Penguin.

Carey, G., and DiLalla, D. L. (1994). Personality and psychopathology: genetic perspectives. *Journal of Abnormal Psychology* 103:32–43.

Cecil, D. (1939). *The Young Melbourne*. London: Constable.

Chess, S., and Thomas, A. (1990). The New York Longitudinal Study: the young adult periods. *Canadian Journal of Psychiatry* 35:557–561.

Chodoff, P. (1982). Hysteria and women. *American Journal of Psychiatry* 139:545–551.

Cloninger, C. R. (1987). A systematic method for clinical description and classification of personality variants. *Archives of General Psychiatry* 44:579–588.

Cloninger, C. R., Svrakic, D. M., and Pryzbeck, T. R. (1993). A psychobiological model of temperament and character. *Archives of General Psychiatry* 50:975–990.

Coccaro, E. F., Siever, L. J., and Klar, H. M. (1989). Serotonergic studies in patients with affective and personality disorders. *Archives of General Psychiatry* 46:587–599.

Collins, A. (1988). *In the Sleep Room*. Toronto: Lester and Orpen Dennys.

Costa, P. T., and Widiger, T. A., eds. (1994). *Personality Disorders and the Five-Factor Model of Personality*. Washington, DC: American Psychological Association.

Dawes, R. (1994). *House of Cards*. New York: Free Press.

Dawson, D., and MacMillan, H. L. (1993). *Relationship Management of the Borderline Patient: From Understanding to Treatment*. New York: Brunner/Mazel.

Dicks, H. V. (1967). *Marital Tensions*. New York: Basic Books.

Dunn, J., and Plomin, R. (1990). *Separate Lives: Why Siblings Are So Different*. New York: Basic Books.

Elkin, I., Shea, T., Watkins, J. T., and Imber, S. D. (1989). National Institute of Mental Health Treatment of Depression Collaborative Research Program: general effectiveness of treatments. *Archives of General Psychiatry* 46:971–982.

Engel, G. L. (1980). The clinical application of the biopsychosocial model. *American Journal of Psychiatry* 137:535–544.

Eysenck, H. (1952). The effects of psychotherapy: an evaluation. *Journal of Consulting Psychology* 16:319–324.

——— (1969). *The Effects of Psychotherapy*. New York: Science House.

——— (1991). Genetic and environmental contributions to individual differences: the three major dimensions of personality. *Journal of Personality* 58:245–261.

Fine, M. A., and Sansone, R. A. (1990). Dilemmas in the management of suicidal behavior in individuals with borderline personality disorder. *American Journal of Psychotherapy* 44:160–171.

Fonagy, P., Leigh, T., Steele, M., et al. (1996). The relation of attachment status, psychiatric classification, and response to psychotherapy. *Journal of Consulting Clinical Psychology* 64:22–31.

Frances, A., Clarkin, J., and Perry, S. (1984). *Differential Therapeutics in Psychiatry*. New York: Brunner/Mazel.

Frances, A. J., and Widiger, T. A. (1985). The classification of personality disorders: an overview of problems and solutions. *Psychiatry Annual Review* 5:240–257. Washington, DC: American Psychiatric Press.

Frank, A. F. (1992). The therapeutic alliances of borderline patients. In *Borderline Personality Disorder: Clinical and Empirical Perspectives*, ed. J. F. Clarkin, E. Marziali, and H. Munroe-Blum, pp. 220–247. New York: Guilford.

Frank, H., and Hoffman, N. (1986). Borderline empathy: an empirical investigation. *Comprehensive Psychiatry* 27:387–395.

Frank, J. D., and Frank, J. B. (1991). *Persuasion and Healing*, 3rd ed. Baltimore: Johns Hopkins University Press.

Freud, S. (1916). A general introduction to psychoanalysis. *Standard Edition* 15, 16:9–463.

——— (1937). Analysis terminable and interminable. *Standard Edition* 23:216–254.

——— (1940). An outline of psychoanalysis. *Standard Edition* 23:144–205.

Fromm-Reichmann, F. (1950). *Principles of Intensive Psychotherapy.* Chicago: University of Chicago Press.

Gabbard, G. O., and Coyne, L. (1987). Predictors of response of antisocial patients to hospital treatment. *Hospital and Community Psychiatry* 38:1181–1185.

Garfield, S. L. (1994). Research on client variables in psychotherapy. In *Handbook of Psychotherapy and Behavior Change*, ed. A. E. Bergin and S. L. Garfield, pp. 190–228. New York: Wiley.

Garmezy, N., and Masten, A. S. (1994). Chronic adversities. In *Child and Adolescent Psychiatry: Modern Approaches*, 3rd ed., ed. M. Rutter and L. Hersov, pp. 191–208. London: Blackwell.

Glantz, K., and Pearce, J. K. (1989). *Exiles from Eden: Psychotherapy from an Evolutional Perspective.* New York: Norton.

Goldstein, R. B., Black, D. D., Nasrallah, A., and Wlnokur, G. (1991). The prediction of suicide: sensitivity, specificity, and predictive value of a multivariate model applied to suicide among 1906 patients with affective disorders. *Archives of General Psychiatry* 48:418–422.

Greben, S. (1984). *Love's Labour.* New York: Schocken.

Greenson, R. (1967). *The Technique and Practice of Psychoanalysis.* New York: International Universities Press.

Gunderson, J. G. (1984). *Borderline Personality Disorder.* Washington, DC: American Psychiatric Press.

—— (1985). Conceptual risks of the Axis I–II division. In *Biological Response Styles: Clinical Implications*, ed. H. Klar and L. J. Siever, pp. 81–95. Washington, DC: American Psychiatric Press.

—— (1994). Narcissistic personality. In *The DSM-IV Personality Disorders*, ed. W. J. Livesley, pp. 201–212. New York: Guilford.

Gunderson, J. G., Frank, A. F., Ronningstam, E. F., et al. (1989). Early discontinuance of borderline patients from psychotherapy. *Journal of Nervous and Mental Disease* 177:38–42.

Gunderson, J. G., and Phillips, K. A. (1991). A current view of the interface between borderline personality disorder and depression. *American Journal of Psychiatry* 148:967–975.

Gunderson, J. G., and Waldinger, R. J. (1987). *Effective Psychotherapy with Borderline Patients.* New York: Macmillan.

Gutheil, T. G. (1989). Borderline personality disorder, boundary violations and patient–therapist sex: medicolegal pitfalls. *American Journal of Psychiatry* 146:597–560.

Gutheil, T. G., and Gabbard, G. O. (1993). The concept of boundaries in clinical practice. *American Journal of Psychiatry* 150:188–196.

Halleck, S. L. (1967). Hysterical personality—psychological, social and iatrogenic determinants. *Archives of General Psychiatry* 16:750–757.

Head, S. B., Baker, J. D., and Williamson, D. A. (1991). Family environment characteristics and dependent personality disorder. *Journal of Personality Disorders* 5:256–263.

Herman, J. (1992). *Trauma and Recovery*. New York: Basic Books.

Herman, J., and van der Kolk, B. (1987). Traumatic antecedents of borderline personality disorder. In *Psychological Trauma*, ed. B. van der Kolk, pp. 11–26. Washington, DC: American Psychiatric Press.

Hetherington, E. M., Cox, M., and Cox, R. (1985). Long-term effects of divorce and remarriage on the adjustment of children. *Journal of the American Academy of Child Psychiatry* 24:518–530.

Hirschfeld, R. M. A., Shea, M. T., and Weise, R. (1991). Dependent personality disorder: perspectives for *DSM-IV*. *Journal of Personality Disorders* 5:135–149.

Hoch, P. H., Cattell, J. P., Strahl, M. D., and Penness, H. H. (1962). The course and outcome of pseudoneurotic schizophrenia. *American Journal of Psychiatry* 119:106–115.

Hogarty, G. E., Anderson, C., Reiss, D., and Kornblith, S. (1991). Family psychoeducation, social skills training and maintenance chemotherapy in the aftercare treatment of schizophrenia. *Archives of General Psychiatry* 48:340–347.

Høglend, D., Sørbye, O., Sorlie, T., et al. (1992). Some criteria for brief dynamic psychotherapy: reliability, factor structure and long-term validity. *Psychotherapy and Psychosomatics* 57:67–74.

Høglend, P. (1993). Personality disorders and long-term outcome after brief dynamic psychotherapy. *Journal of Personality Disorders* 7:168–181.

Hollender, M. H. (1971). Hysterical personality. *Comments on Contemporary Psychiatry* 1:17–23.

Horowitz, M. J. (1986). *Stress Response Syndromes*. Northvale, NJ: Jason Aronson.

Horwitz, L. (1974). *Clinical Prediction in Psychotherapy*. New York: Jason Aronson.

Howard, K. I., Kopta, A. M., Krause, M. S., and Orlinsky, D. E. (1986). The dose-effect relationship to psychotherapy. *American Psychologist* 41:159–164.

Hull, J. W., Yeomans, F., Clarkin, J., et al. (1996). Factors associated with multiple hospitalizations of patients with borderline personality disorder. *Psychiatric Services* 47:638–641.

Hwu, H. G., Yeh, E. K., and Change, L. Y. (1989). Prevalence of psychiatric disorders in Taiwan defined by the Chinese Diagnostic Interview Schedule. *Acta Psychiatrica Scandinavica* 79:136–147.

Jacobsen, N., and Gurman, A., eds. (1995). *Clinical Handbook of Couple Therapy*. New York: Guilford.

Jung, C. G. (1920). *Psychological Types*. Princeton: Princeton University Press, 1971.

Kagan, J. (1994). *Galen's Prophecy*. New York: Basic Books.

Kaufman, C., Grunebaum, H., Cohler, B., and Gamer, E. (1979). Superkids: competent children of schizophrenic mothers. *American Journal of Psychiatry* 136:1398–1402.

Keitner, I. G., and Miller, I. W. (1990). Family functioning and major depression: an overview. *American Journal of Psychiatry* 147:1128–1137.

Kendler, K. S. (1995). Genetic epidemiology in psychiatry: taking both genes and environment seriously. *Archives of General Psychiatry* 52:895–899.

——— (1996). Parenting: a genetic epidemiological perspective. *American Journal of Psychiatry* 153:11–20.

Kernberg, O. F. (1974). Barriers to falling and remaining in love. *Journal of the American Psychoanalytic Association* 22:743–760.

——— (1976). *Borderline Conditions and Pathological Narcissism*. New York: Jason Aronson.

——— (1984). *Severe Personality Disorders*. New Haven: Yale University Press.

Kernberg, O. F., Coyne, L., Appelbaum, A., et al. (1972). Final report of the Menninger Psychotherapy Research Project. *Bulletin of the Menninger Clinic* 36:1–275.

Kirmayer, L. J., Robbins, J. M., and Paris, J. (1994). Somatoform disorders: personality and the social matrix of somatic distress. *Journal of Abnormal Psychology* 103:125–136.

Klein, M. (1946). *Envy and Gratitude.* New York: International Universities Press.

Klerman, G. L., and Weissman, M., eds. (1993). *New Applications of Interpersonal Psychotherapy.* Washington, DC: American Psychiatric Press.

Kohut, H. (1970). *The Analysis of the Self.* New York: International Universities Press.

——— (1977). *The Restoration of the Self.* New York: International Universities Press.

——— (1984). *How Does Analysis Cure?* Chicago: University of Chicago Press.

Kopta, S. M., Howard, K. I., Lowry, J. L., and Beutler, L. E. (1994). Patterns of symptomatic recovery in psychotherapy. *Journal of Consulting Clinical Psychology* 62:1009–1016.

Kramer, P. (1993). *Listening to Prozac.* New York: Viking.

Krohn, A. (1974). Borderline "empathy" and differentiation of object representations. *International Journal of Psychoanalytic Psychotherapy* 3:142–165.

Kroll, J. (1988). *The Challenge of the Borderline Patient.* New York: Norton.

——— (1993). *PTSD/Borderlines in Therapy.* New York: Norton.

Labonté, E., and Paris, J. (1993). Life stress in borderline personality disorder. *Canadian Journal of Psychiatry* 38:638–640.

Lambert, M. J. (1992). Psychotherapy outcome research: implications for integrative and eclectic treatment. In *Handbook of Psychotherapy Integration,* ed. J. C. Norcross and M. C. Goldfried, pp. 94–129. New York: Basic Books.

Lambert, M. J., and Bergin, A. E. (1994). The effectiveness of psychotherapy. In *Handbook of Psychotherapy and Behavior Change,* ed. A. E. Bergin and S. L. Garfield, pp. 143–189. New York: Wiley.

Lansky, M. R. (1991). Shame and fragmentation in the marital dyad. *Contemporary Family Therapy* 13:17–31.

Lasch, C. (1979). *The Culture of Narcissism.* New York: Warner.

Lazarus, R. S., and Folkman, S. (1984). *Stress, Appraisal and Coping.* New York: Springer.

Lehmann, H. (1975). Clinical features of schizophrenia. In *Comprehen-*

sive Textbook of Psychiatry, ed. A. Freedman, H. Kaplan, and B. Sadock, pp. 890–922. Baltimore: Williams & Wilkins.

Leibenluft, E., Gardner, D. L., and Cowdry, R. W. (1987). The inner experience of the borderline self-mutilator. *Journal of Personality Disorders* 1:317–324.

Leighton, D. C., Harding, J. S., and Macklin, D. B. (1963). *The Character of Danger: Psychiatric Symptoms in Selected Communities*. New York: Basic Books.

Lerner, D. (1958). *The Passing of Traditional Society*. New York: Free Press.

Lerner, H. E. (1974). The hysterical personality: a "woman's disease." *Comprehensive Psychiatry* 15:157–164.

Levy, D. M. (1943). *Maternal Overprotection*. New York: Columbia University Press.

Lewis, L., and Appleby, L. (1988). Personality disorders: the patients psychiatrists dislike. *British Journal of Psychiatry* 153:44–49.

Linehan, M. M. (1993). *Cognitive-Behavioral Treatment of Borderline Personality Disorder*. New York: Guilford.

Links, P. S., Steiner, B., and Huxley, G. (1988). The occurrence of borderline personality disorder in the families of borderline patients. *Journal of Personality Disorders* 2:14–20.

Livesley, W. J., Jang, K., Schroeder, M. L., and Jackson, D. N. (1993). Genetic and environmental factors in personality dimensions. *American Journal of Psychiatry* 150:1826–1831.

Livesley, W. J., Schroeder, M. L., Jackson, D. N., and Jang, K. (1994). Categorical distinctions in the study of personality disorder: implications for classification. *Journal of Abnormal Psychology* 103:6–17.

Loranger, A. W. (1991). Comorbidity of borderline disorder in 5000 patients. Paper presented to the American Psychiatric Association, New Orleans, May.

Loranger, A. W., Sartori, N., Andreoli, A., et al. (1994). The International Personality Disorder Examination. *Archives of General Psychiatry* 51:215–224.

Luborsky, L., Crits-Christoph, P., Mintz, J., and Auerbach, A. (1988). *Who Will Benefit from Psychotherapy? Predicting Therapeutic Outcomes*. New York: Basic Books.

Luborsky, L., and Crits-Christoph, P. (1990). *Understanding Transfer-*

ence: The Core Conflict Relationship Theme Method. New York: Basic Books.

Luborsky, L., Singer, B., and Luborsky, L. (1975). Comparative studies of psychotherapy: Is it true that "everyone has won and all shall have prizes"? Archives of General Psychiatry 41:165–180.

Lykken, D. T., McGue, M., Tellegen, A., and Boucard, T. J. (1992). Emergenesis: genetic traits which may not run in families. American Psychologist 47:1565–1577.

Malan, D. (1979). Individual Psychotherapy and the Science of Psychodynamics. Boston: Butterworth.

Malinovsky-Rummell, R., and Hansen, D. J. (1993). Long-term consequences of physical abuse. Psychological Bulletin 114:68–79.

Maltsberger, J. T., and Buie, D. (1973). Countertransference hate in the treatment of suicidal patients. Archives of General Psychiatry 30:625–633.

Markowitz, P. J. (1993). SSRI treatment of borderline personality. Paper presented to the meeting of the International Society for the Study of Personality Disorders, Cambridge, MA, September.

Mascie-Taylor, C. G. (1989). Spouse similarity for IQ and personality and convergence. Behavior Genetics 19:223–227.

Masters, R. D., and McGuire, M. T. (1994). The Neurotransmitter Revolution: Serotonin, Social Behavior, and the Law. Carbondale, IL: Southern Illinois University Press.

Maziade, M., Caron, C., Coté, R., et al. (1990). Extreme temperament and diagnosis: a study in a psychiatric sample of consecutive children. Archives of General Psychiatry 47:477–484.

McCrae, R. R., and Costa, P. T. (1990). Personality in Adulthood. New York: Guilford.

McGlashan, T. H. (1993). Implications of outcome research for the treatment of borderline personality disorder. In Borderline Personality Disorder: Etiology and Treatment, ed. J. Paris, pp. 235–260. Washington, DC: American Psychiatric Press.

McGuffin, P., and Thapar, A. (1992). The genetics of personality disorder. British Journal of Psychiatry 160:12–23.

Miller, A. (1981). Prisoners of Childhood, trans. R. Ward. New York: Basic Books.

Millon, T. (1987). On the genesis and prevalence of borderline personality disorder: a social learning thesis. *Journal of Personality Disorders* 1:354–372.

—— (1993). Borderline personality disorder: a psychosocial epidemic. In *Borderline Personality Disorder: Etiology and Treatment*, ed. J. Paris, pp. 197–210. Washington, DC: American Psychiatric Press.

Millon, T., and Davis, R. (1996). *Personality Disorders: DSM-IV and Beyond*. New York: Wiley.

Minuchin, S. (1974). *Families and Family Therapy*. Cambridge: Harvard University Press.

Monsen, J. T., Odland, T., Faugli, A., et al. (1995). Personality disorders: changes and stability after intensive psychotherapy focusing on affect consciousness. *Psychotherapy Research* 5:33–48.

Mora, G. L. (1975). Historical and theoretical trends in psychiatry. In *Comprehensive Textbook of Psychiatry*, ed. A. Freedman, H. Kaplan, and B. Sadock, 2nd ed., pp. 1–75. Baltimore: Williams & Wilkins.

Mulder, R. T. (1991). Personality disorders in New Zealand hospitals. *Acta Psychiatrica Scandinavica* 84:197–202.

Murdoch, I. (1983). *The Philosopher's Pupil*. London: Chatto and Windus.

Najavits, L. M., and Gunderson, J. G. (1995). Better than expected: improvements in borderline personality disorder in a 3-year prospective outcome study. *Comprehensive Psychiatry* 36:296–302.

Nakao, K., Gunderson, J. G., Phillips, K. A., et al. (1992). Functional impairment in personality disorders. *Journal of Personality Disorders* 6:24–33.

Nestadt, G., Romanovski, A. J., Chahal, R., et al. (1990). An epidemiological study of histrionic personality disorder. *Psychological Medicine* 20:413–422.

Nigg, J. T., and Goldsmith, H. H. (1994). Genetics of personality disorders: perspectives from personality and psychopathology research. *Psychological Bulletin* 115:346–380.

Nin, A. (1966). *The Diary of Anais Nin*, volume I. New York: Harcourt Brace World.

Oldham, J. M., Skodol, A. E., Kellman, D., et al. (1992). Diagnosis of *DSM-III-R* personality disorders by two structured interviews:

patterns of comorbidity. *American Journal of Psychiatry* 149:213–220.

—— (1995). Comorbidity of Axis I and Axis II disorders. *American Journal of Psychiatry* 152:571–578.

Orlinsky, D. E., Grawe, K., and Parks, B. K. (1994). Process and outcome in psychotherapy—noch einmal. In *Handbook of Psychotherapy and Behavior Change*, ed. A. E. Bergin and S. L. Garfield, pp. 270–379. New York: Wiley.

Paris, J. (1988). Long-term outcome of borderline personality disorder: a critical review. *Journal of Personality Disorders* 2:189–197.

—— (1993a). Treatment of borderline personality disorder in the light of the research on its long-term outcome. *Canadian Journal of Psychiatry* 38:S28–34.

—— (1993b). Personality disorders: a biopsychosocial model. *Journal of Personality Disorders* 7:255–264.

—— (1994). *Borderline Personality Disorder: A Multidimensional Approach.* Washington, DC: American Psychiatric Press.

—— (1995). Memories of abuse in BPD: True or false? *Harvard Review of Psychiatry* 3:10–17.

—— (1996). *Social Factors in the Personality Disorders: A Biopsychosocial Approach to Etiology and Treatment.* New York: Cambridge University Press.

—— (1997a). Childhood trauma as an etiological factor in the personality disorders. *Journal of Personality Disorders* 11:34–49.

—— (1997b). Antisocial and borderline personality disorders: Two separate diagnoses or two aspects of the same psychopathology? *Comprehensive Psychiatry* 38.

—— (in press). *Nature and Nurture in Psychiatry: A Predisposition-stress Model of Mental Disorders.* Washington, DC: American Psychiatric Press.

Paris, J., Brown, R., and Nowlis, D. (1987). Long-term follow-up of borderline patients in a general hospital. *Comprehensive Psychiatry* 28:530–535.

Paris, J., Frank, H., Buonvino, M., and Bond, M. (1991). Recollections of parental behavior and Axis II cluster diagnosis. *Journal of Personality Disorders* 5:102–106.

Paris, J., Zweig-Frank, H., Bond, M., and Guzder, J. (1996). Defense styles, hostility, and psychological risk factors in male patients with personality disorders. *Journal of Nervous and Mental Disease* 184:155–160.

Parker, G. (1983). *Parental Overprotection: A Risk Factor in Psychosocial Development.* New York: Grune & Stratton.

Peck, S. (1985). *The Road Less Traveled.* New York: Simon and Schuster.

Perry, J. C. (1993). Longitudinal studies of personality disorders. *Journal of Personality Disorders* Supp. 63–85.

Perry, J. C., and Cooper, S. H. (1989). An empirical study of defense mechanisms. *Archives of General Psychiatry* 46:444–452.

Pilkonis, P. A., and Frank, E. (1988). Personality pathology in recurrent depression: nature, prevalence, and relationship to treatment response. *American Journal of Psychiatry* 144:485–488.

Piper, W. E., Azim, H. A., Joyce, A. S., and McCallum, M. (1991). Transference interpretations, therapeutic alliance, and outcome in short-term individual psychotherapy. *Archives of General Psychiatry* 48:946–953.

Piper, W. E., Rosie, J. S., and Joyce, A. S. (1996). *Time-Limited Day Treatment for Personality Disorders: Integration of Research and Practice in a Group Program.* Washington, DC: American Psychological Association.

Plomin, R., DeFries, J. C., and McClearn, G. E. (1990). *Behavioral Genetics: A Primer.* New York: W. H. Freeman.

Pokorny, A. D. (1982). Prediction of suicide in psychiatric patients: report of a prospective study. *Archives of General Psychiatry* 40:249–257.

Propst, A., Paris, J., and Rosberger, Z. (1994). Do therapist experience, diagnosis and functional level predict outcome in short-term psychotherapy? *Canadian Journal of Psychiatry* 39:178–183.

Proust, M. (1913, translation 1992). *Swann's Way,* trans. C. K. Scott Moncrieff, T. Kilmartin, and D. J. Enright. New York: Modern Library.

Reich, J. (1990). Relationship between *DSM-III* avoidant and dependent personality disorders. *Psychiatry Research* 34:281–292.

Reich, W. (1933). *Character Analysis.* New York: Farrar, Straus, & Giroux, 1972.

Reich, J., Yates, W., and Nduaguba, M. (1989). Prevalence of *DSM-III* personality disorders in the community. *Social Psychiatry and Psychiatric Epidemiology* 24:12–16.

Reiss, D., Plomin, R., and Hetherington, E. M. (1992). Genetics and psychiatry: an unheralded window on the environment. *American Journal of Psychiatry* 149:147–155.

Riley, G. (1991). *Divorce: An American Tradition.* New York: Oxford University Press.

Robins, L. N. (1966). *Deviant Children Grown Up.* Baltimore: Williams & Wilkins.

Rockland, L. H. (1992). *Supportive Therapy for Borderline Patients: A Dynamic Approach.* New York: Guilford.

Roethlisberger, F. J., and Dickson, W. J. (1939). *Management and the Work Place.* Cambridge: Harvard University Press.

Rogers, C. (1961). *On Becoming A Person.* New York: Houghton Mifflin.

Rosen, J. (1953). *Direct Analysis.* New York: Grune & Stratton.

Rothbart, M. K., and Ahadi, S. A. (1994). Temperament and the development of personality. *Journal of Abnormal Psychology* 103:55–66.

Rutter, M. (1987). Temperament, personality, and personality development. *British Journal of Psychiatry* 150:443–448.

——— (1989). Pathways from childhood to adult life. *Journal of Child Psychology and Psychiatry* 30:23–51.

Rutter, M., and Maughan, B. (1997). Psychosocial adversities in psychopathology. *Journal of Personality Disorders* 11:4–18.

Rutter, M., and Quinton, D. (1984). Long-term follow-up of women institutionalized in childhood. *British Journal of Developmental Psychology* 18:225–234.

Rutter, M., and Rutter, M. (1993). *Developing Minds: Challenge and Continuity Across the Life Span.* New York: Basic Books.

Ryle, A. (1997). The structure and development of borderline personality: a proposed model. *British Journal of Psychiatry* 170:82–87.

Sabo, A. N., Gunderson, J. G., Najavits, L. M., et al. (1995). Changes in self-destructiveness of borderline patients in psychotherapy: a prospective follow up. *Journal of Nervous and Mental Disease* 183:370–376.

Salzman, L. (1968). *The Obsessive Personality.* New York: Science House.

Sato, T., and Takeichi, M. (1993). Lifetime prevalence of specific psychiatric disorders in a general medicine clinic. *General Hospital Psychiatry* 15:224–233.

Scarr, S., and McCartney, K. (1983). How people make their own environments: a theory of genotype-environment effects. *Child Development* 54:424–435.

Schlesinger, L. (1996). *You Can't Do That*. New York: Harper Collins.

Schmideberg, M. (1959). The borderline patient. In *The American Handbook of Psychiatry*, ed. S. Arieti, I:398–416. New York: Basic Books.

Seligman, M. E. P. (1995). The effectiveness of psychotherapy: the *Consumer Reports* study. *American Psychologist* 50:965–974.

Shapiro, D. (1965). *Neurotic Styles*. New York: Basic Books.

Shea, M. T., Pilkonis, P. A., Beckham, E., et al. (1990). Personality disorders and treatment outcome in the NIMH Treatment of Depression Collaborative Research Program. *American Journal of Psychiatry* 147:711–718.

Shea, M. T., Widiger, T. A., and Klein, M. H. (1992). Comorbidity of personality disorders and depression: implications for treatment. *Journal of Consulting Clinical Psychology* 60:857–868.

Siever, L. J., and Davis, L. (1991). A psychobiological perspective on the personality disorders. *American Journal of Psychiatry* 148:1647–1658.

Silver, D. (1983). Psychotherapy of the characterologically difficult patient. *Canadian Journal of Psychiatry* 28:513–521.

Skodol, A. E., Buckley, P., and Charles, E. (1983). Is there a characteristic pattern in the treatment history of clinic outpatients with borderline personality? *Journal of Nervous and Mental Disease* 171:405–410.

Slavney, P. R., and McHugh, P. R. (1974). The hysterical personality: a controlled study. *Archives of General Psychiatry* 30:325–329.

Slyper, A., and Schectman, G. (1994). Coronary artery disease risk factors from a genetic and developmental perspective. *Archives of Internal Medicine* 154:633–638.

Smith, M. L., Glass, G. V., and Miller, T. I. (1980). *The Benefits of Psychotherapy*. Baltimore: Johns Hopkins University Press.

Soloff, P. H. (1993). Psychopharmacological intervention in borderline personality disorder. In *Borderline Personality Disorder: Etiology and Treatment*, ed. J. Paris, pp. 319–348. Washington, DC: American Psychiatric Press.

Spence, D. (1983). *Narrative Truth and Historical Truth*. New York: Norton.

Stern, A. (1938). Psychoanalytic investigation of and therapy in the borderline group of neuroses. *Psychoanalytic Quarterly* 7:467–489.

Stevenson, J., and Meares, R. (1992). An outcome study of psychotherapy for patients with borderline personality disorder. *American Journal of Psychiatry* 149:358–362.

Stone, M. H. (1980). *The Borderline Syndromes*. New York: McGraw Hill.

——— (1990). *The Fate of Borderline Patients*. New York: Guilford.

——— (1993). *Abnormalities of Personality*. New York: Norton.

Storr, A. (1988). *Solitude*. New York: Free Press.

Strupp, H. H., Fox, R. S., and Lesser, K. (1969). *Patients View Their Psychotherapy*. Baltimore: Johns Hopkins University Press.

Strupp, H. H., and Hadley, S. W. (1979). Specific vs. non-specific factors in psychotherapy. *Archives of General Psychiatry* 36:1125–1136.

Storr, A. (1988). *Solitude*. New York: Free Press.

Stravynski, A., Belisle, M., Macouiller, M., et al. (1994). The treatment of avoidant personality disorder by social skills training in the clinic or in real-life settings. *Canadian Journal of Psychiatry* 39:377–383.

Sulloway, F. (1996). *Born to Rebel*. New York: Pantheon.

Swenson, C. (1995). Dialectical Behavior Therapy for Suicidal Borderline Patients. Paper presented to the 6th Annual Summer Session of the American Association of Suicidology, Santa Fe, New Mexico, July.

Taylor, C. (1992). *The Malaise of Modernity*. Toronto: Anisna.

Tellegen, A., Lykken, D. T., Bouchard, T. J., et al. (1988). Personality similarity in twins reared apart and together. *Journal of Personality and Social Psychology* 54:1031–1039.

Tennant, C. (1988). Parental loss in childhood to adult life. *Archives of General Psychiatry* 45:1045–1050.

Thomas, A., and Chess, C. (1977). *Temperament and Development*. New York: Brunner/Mazel.

Torgersen, S. (1980). The oral, obsessive and hysterical personality syndromes: a study of heredity and environmental factors by means of the twin method. *Archives of General Psychiatry* 37:1272–1277.

—— (1983). Genetic factors in anxiety disorders. *Archives of General Psychiatry* 40:1085–1089.

—— (1984). Genetic and nosological aspects of schizotypal and borderline personality disorders: a twin study. *Archives of General Psychiatry* 41:546–554.

—— (1995). Correlates of Personality Disorder Diagnoses. Paper presented at the meeting of the International Society for the Study of Personality Disorders, Dublin, June.

—— (1996). Personality disorders in our genes? Paper presented at the meeting of the Second European Congress on Personality Disorders, Milan, June.

Tyrer, P. (1988). *Personality Disorders*. London: Wright.

Vaillant, G. E. (1977). *Adaptation to Life*. Boston: Little, Brown.

Vaillant, G. E., and Vaillant, C. O. (1990). Natural history of male psychological health, XII: a 45-year study of predictors of successful aging at age 65. *American Journal of Psychiatry* 147:31–37.

Valenstein, E. S. (1986). *Great and Desperate Measures*. New York: Basic Books.

van Reekum, R., Links, P. S., and Boiago, I. (1993). Constitutional factors in borderline personality disorder. In *Borderline Personality Disorder*, ed. J. Paris, pp. 13–38. Washington, DC: American Psychiatric Press.

Varenne, H. (1996). Love and liberty: the contemporary American family. In *A History of the Family: Volume II*, ed. A. Burguière, C. Kalpisch-Zuber, M. Segalen, and F. Zonabend, pp. 416–441. Cambridge: Belknap.

Wachtel, P. L. (1977). *Psychoanalysis and Behavior Therapy*. New York: Basic Books.

—— (1993). *Therapeutic Communication*. New York: Guilford.

—— (1994). Cyclical processes in personality and psychopathology. *Journal of Abnormal Psychology* 103:51–54.

Waldinger, R. J. (1987). Intensive psychodynamic therapy with borderline patients: an overview. *American Journal of Psychiatry* 144:267–274.

Waldinger, R. J., and Gunderson, J. G. (1984). Completed psychotherapies with borderline patients. *American Journal of Psychotherapy* 38:190–201.

Wallerstein, J. (1989). *Second Chances: Men, Women, and Children a Decade After Divorce.* New York: Ticknor and Fields.

Wallerstein, R. (1986). *Forty-two Lives in Treatment.* New York: Guilford.

Werner, E. E., and Smith, R. S. (1992). *Overcoming the Odds: High Risk Children from Birth to Adulthood.* New York: Cornell University Press.

West, M. O., and Prinz, R. J. (1987). Parental alcoholism and childhood psychopathology. *Psychological Bulletin* 102:204–224.

Westen, D. (1985). *Self and Society: Narcissism, Collectivism and the Development of Morals.* New York: Cambridge University Press.

Widiger, T. A., Trull, T. J., Clarkin, J. F., et al. (1994). A description of the *DSM-III-R* and *DSM-IV* personality disorders with the five factor model of personality. In *Personality Disorders and the Five Factor Model*, ed. P. T. Costa and T. A. Widiger, pp. 41–58. Washington, DC: American Psychological Association.

Winnicott, D. W. (1958). Psychoses and child care. In *Collected Papers*, pp. 219–228. London: Tavistock.

——— (1965). The capacity to be alone. In *The Maturational Processes and the Facilitating Environment*, pp. 29–38. New York: International Universities Press.

Winston, A., Laikin, M., Pollack, J., et al. (1994). Short-term psychotherapy of personality disorders. *American Journal of Psychiatry* 151:190–194.

Yeomans, F., Selzer, M., and Clarkin, J. F. (1992). *Treating the Borderline Patient: A Contract-Based Approach.* New York: Basic Books.

Yochelson, S., and Samenow, S. (1976). *The Criminal Personality*, vol. I. New York: Jason Aronson.

Zanarini, M. C. (1993). Borderline personality as an impulse spectrum disorder. In *Borderline Personality Disorder: Etiology and Treatment*, ed. J. Paris, pp. 67–86. Washington, DC: American Psychiatric Press.

Zanarini, M. C., Gunderson, J. G., and Frankenburg, F. R. (1990). Cognitive features of borderline personality disorder. *American Journal of Psychiatry* 147:57–63.

Zanarini, M. C., and Frankenburg, F. R. (1994). Emotional hypochondriasis, hyperbole, and the borderline patient. *Journal of Psychotherapy Practice and Research* 3:25–36.

Zetzel, E. (1970). The so-called good hysteric. In *The Capacity for Emotional Growth*, pp. 229–245. New York: International Universities Press.

——— (1971). A developmental approach to the borderline patient. *American Journal of Psychiatry* 127:867–871.

Zweig-Frank, H., and Paris, J. (1995). The five factor model of personality in borderline personality disorder. *Canadian Journal of Psychiatry* 40:523–526.

Index